ON WINGS

Mark Weis

Mark Weis
On Wings of Eagles

For my dad.

Sixty-five years ago, you gave me
a home, name, and family.
I've never met anyone more selfless or loving.
In you I glimpsed the meaning
of having a "Father" in heaven.

I love and miss you.

With Gratitude

Many thanks to Craig F. Owings
for reviewing and editing this book.
I am fortunate to have an
experienced English teacher
as a dear friend and editor.
Blessings to you and yours.

Many thanks also to my dear friend, colleague,
and mentor, Rollin Reim.
Your ministry and love for the Gospel
greatly inspired me.
I'm forever in your debt.

Forward

When I was a boy, my dad taught me the time-honored phrase *tempus fugit*, which is Latin for "time flees." I didn't understand the concept then; however, as a man approaching the age of sixty-five, I do understand now.

It is hard for me to believe that I started this collection of poems and devotions in 1991. That was twenty-seven years ago; and frankly, a long time to let anything simmer on the burner. For perspective, when I wrote the first words of this book, my son Justin was only three, and my son Andrew was not yet born. Justin is now twenty-nine. Andrew is twenty-five.

And as time has *fugited*, my life has changed in other ways too: two unwanted divorces, three corporate downsizings, bankruptcy, automobile accidents, cancer surgeries, and the death of loved ones. Unavoidably, and perhaps appropriately, I've incorporated some of my personal experiences into this book.

But *On Wings of Eagles* is not about me. Instead, it is about the grace and power of God at work in my life: the God who saved me in spite of me, rescued me when I wondered and wandered, and picked me up the many times I've fallen.

The apostle Paul told the Christians in Rome, "For whatever things were written before were written for our learning, that we through the patience and comfort of the Scriptures might have hope." This is why *On Wings of*

Eagles is based on Scripture and not on me—that you, dear reader, might have hope.

In the meanwhile, here is another Latin phrase to remember: *Soli Deo Gloria.* It means "to God alone be glory."

And let the congregation say, "Amen."

"You have seen what I did to the Egyptians,
and how I bore you on eagles' wings
and brought you to Myself." Exodus 19:4

"But those who wait on the LORD
Shall renew their strength;
They shall mount up with wings like eagles,
They shall run and not be weary,
They shall walk and not faint." Isaiah 40:31

Contents

No Miracles Allowed

"Now He did not do many mighty works there
because of their unbelief." Matthew 13:58

I have always found this Bible verse startling and
remarkably sad. The inhabitants of most towns Jesus
visited were desperate for His miracles. They laid the sick
at His feet. They followed Him into the countryside with
no thought of food or lodging. They yearned to touch even
the hem of His garments.

However, such was not the case in Nazareth, the
hometown of Jesus. Of Nazareth we read, "Now He did not
do many mighty works there." Why would the Nazarenes
spurn Christ's miracles, when so many of us pray for
miracles in our lives? "Jesus, save my marriage." "Jesus,
heal my illness." "Jesus, help me find a job." "Jesus, don't
let my loved one die."

Why would the people of Nazareth, figuratively speaking,
post *NO MIRACLES ALLOWED* signs all over town?
Matthew explained, "...because of their unbelief." Though
fully aware of Christ's power to work miracles, many in
Nazareth were offended (literally "scandalized") by His
humble appearance and hometown origin. They refused to
believe that the son of a lowly carpenter could also be the
Son of the Living God.

Jesus has the power and willingness to work miracles in
our lives, too. Are we willing to let Him?

There is a place where God does no miracles,
where water is never made wine,
where the lame do not walk,
the mute do not talk,
and the sightless prefer to stay blind.

The deaf never hear when the Savior draws near,
the Lord of life and creation.
The found remain lost,
spurning the cost
of their perfectly completed salvation.

The self-righteous do not see what is certain to be,
blind to their hopeless condition.
The infirm still think
they're too whole to be sick,
and see no need for the Good Physician.

Here no sinner repents, no mourner laments,
the dead are not raised from the grave.
No leper is cleansed,
no foe is made friend.
The forgiven refused to be saved.

What place is this with so much amiss,
with laughter to cover cold grief?
This place of the proud—
NO MIRACLES ALLOWED—
is a place called "Unbelief."

God on a Shelf

"Can a virgin forget her ornaments, or a bride her attire?
Yet My people have forgotten Me
days without number." Jeremiah 2:32

In 1976 I visited Israel with a group of Christian friends. We swam in the Sea of Galilee, read the Beatitudes on the slope where Jesus delivered His Sermon on the Mount, and marveled at Golgotha, Gethsemane, and the Garden Tomb.

While in Nazareth, I purchased an olivewood statue of Jesus. The statue was hand-carved and intricately detailed. I was fascinated by the look of compassion on Christ's face, the flow of His hair and robe, and the way His palms were open in benediction. Of all the mementos I brought back from that trip, the olivewood statue of Jesus was my favorite.

Over time, however, the scent of the olivewood faded, and so did my interest in the statue. My once-prized possession became just one more dust-covered fixture in my study, its hands raised in blessing over a Hebrew lexicon and a novel by Stephen King.

Then one day, while dusting the statue, I had a terrible thought. How often had I treated the real Jesus in the same way: ignoring Him until I needed Him, and then returning Him to the "shelf" of my indifference once my problem was solved?

How amazing that God loves us and answers us when we call on Him. Yet, I wonder how much our indifference and ingratitude hurt Him? There is unmistakable sorrow in the words, "Yet My people have forgotten Me days without number."

GOD ON A SHELF

Olivewood Jesus on my shelf,
dusty, musty, all by Yourself,
sculpted feet, arms raised in blessing
over books and nooks and window dressings.

Now and then I take you down
to dust, adjust, and move around.
When I'm through with You I put You back
to guard my shelves of Fiction and Fact.

And more than once I'd have to say,
"I've treated the real Jesus in just the same way."

Row, Row, Row Your Boat

"But the boat was now in the middle
of the sea, tossed by the waves,
for the wind was contrary." Matthew 14:24

Few Bible stories are more familiar than Jesus walking on water and calming the raging storm on Lake Galilee. Not only are the images striking—blustering winds, punishing waves, a boat pitching and yawing like a child's plaything—the storm itself is a perfect metaphor for the unforeseen problems of life.

Storms come in all shapes and sizes. Some have nothing to do with the weather, but are just as unpredictable and destructive, crashing over us like white-capped breakers and threatening to shipwreck our faith. These storms also have names: Hurricane Sickness. Tsunami Divorce. Typhoon Debt. Tornado Doubt. Cyclone Death.

Amid all the storms of life, both literal and figurative, it is vital that we keep the eyes of our faith wide open and focused on Jesus; that we disregard the size of the waves and the force of the winds, and recognize Jesus as He truly is: the Almighty God, the Master of Wind and Wave, the compassionate Savior who calms our troubled lives as easily as He calmed the troubled lake.

At times, it may actually take a storm to focus our faith on Jesus. Easily overlooked in this Bible account is the fact that Jesus Himself directed His disciples to cross the lake—into a storm that He saw coming.

ROW, ROW, ROW YOUR BOAT

You knew the storm was coming, Lord.
You knew, and still sent me out to meet it
with my miserable little boat
and puny wooden oars.

You looked at me searchingly
(the look that always makes me wonder what You see),
then smiled and said,
"Get into the boat and cross the lake.
I'll meet you on the other side."

Grinning, I stood there thinking
it such a fine day for sailing:
the cloudless blue sky,
the lazy summer breeze,
the azure water licking my feet.

Eagerly I stepped into the boat,
slipping in my haste
(did I thank You for catching me?),
forgetting even to wave goodbye.

You knew the storm was coming, Lord.
Yet, You pushed me off.
Hand shielding brows,
You watched me row toward the center of the lake,
where I stowed my oars,
glad for the sun on my cheeks,
content to drift in the gentle current.

I didn't tell You then
(though I suspect You knew)
that I was happy to be away from the crowds,
the noise, the work, even You.
There were some things I needed to do alone,
like crossing a calm lake.

Suddenly, the storm hit,
brutal and maniacal in its force.
In an instant everything turned against me:
the sky, now black and swollen;
the summer wind, now a blustering gale;
the azure water, now a boiling cauldron,
tossing me effortlessly like a child's toy.

You sent me out into that storm, Lord.
You did.
And when it struck, I turned.
I looked for You.
I screamed Your name,
but You were gone.

Cold with panic, I seized the oars.
With back bent and feet planted,
I rowed, rowed, rowed
against the storm,
against the howling wind and punishing waves,
against the pelting rain—
and lost ground with every stroke.

Hours passed. Hours!
And with every one spent battling that storm

my arms grew wearier, my back sorer,
my hands bloodier, my destination farther.

And in one blinding, deafening bolt of insight
I understood that I would die,
alone, Savior-less,
in a storm You saw coming.

That is when You came to me,
walking on water,
the Master of Wind and Wave.

That is when You said to me,
"Why is your faith so small?"
And to the storm,
"Hush now! Be quiet!"

That is when calm came to my troubled soul
and to the troubled lake.

That is when You stepped into my boat
(did I thank You for coming?),
and You and I together,
without one stroke of an oar,
instantly reached the opposite shore.

You knew that the storm was coming, Lord.
You knew.
Yet, You sent me out to meet it, to learn from it,
that whether calm, quiet moments
or foul, hostile weather,
I am never, ever alone.

I'm No Abraham

"And he believed in the LORD, and He accounted
it to him as righteousness." Genesis 15:6

I have always marveled at the faith of Abraham. Here was a man whom God told to leave the safe and familiar, and to travel to a place he would be shown. He had no roadmap, no directions, and no clear destination. Yet, without asking where or why, Abraham packed his family and belongings and did as God directed.

When Abraham was ninety years old, his body reproductively dead, his wife barren, God promised him that he would not only father a son, but that his descendants would be as numerous as the stars.

Abraham waited another ten years for God to fulfill this promise. He would have thought of it each time he felt an ache in his old bones, or gazed at the constellations, or even heard his own name. Abraham means "father of many." Yet the Bible states that, despite the delays and human impossibilities, Abraham "believed in the LORD, and He accounted it to him as righteousness."

I'm no Abraham. Few of us are. But when we marvel at this man of faith, it is important to remember that his ability to walk unswervingly into the unknown was not due to his own strength or righteousness. It was due to his unshakable belief in the utter faithfulness of God.

I'M NO ABRAHAM

Lord, I'm no Abraham,
that man of faith who in the autumn of his life
left home, relatives, the affairs of heart,
and walked unswervingly toward a land called Promise;
never stumbling, never faltering,
never regretting his decision,
always seeing the hidden,
always expecting the impossible.

How? I wonder.

Had You asked me to leave my home,
I'd have said, "But the market is depressed.
The house won't sell."

Had You pointed me toward an unknown land,
I'd have said, "But the car needs a tune-up.
And I don't have a map."

Had You
(how could You?)
demanded the life of my son,
I'd have paled, wailed, gasped, blanched,
and told You in no uncertain terms,
"The life of my son is nothing to joke about!
He's only three, You know."

I'm no Abraham.
But for every halting, stumbling step
I take toward the Land of Promise,

for every worthless piece of luggage I leave behind,
for even the most microscopic sacrifice I make
for the Savior's sake,
how thankful I am that You
are unchangeably the same God.

Goliath on the Horizon

"You come to me with a sword, with a spear, and with a javelin. But I come to you in the name of the LORD of hosts." 1 Samuel 17:45

For forty days Goliath dared any soldier in the Israelite army to fight him. No one accepted his challenge. Every Israelite soldier in the camp, including King Saul, cowered at the giant's words and size.

Then one day, young David arrived at the camp to visit his older brothers. When he heard Goliath's taunts, he was incensed. "For who is this uncircumcised Philistine," he asked, "that he should defy the armies of the living God?" (1 Samuel 17:26) Against all odds and advice, David insisted on fighting Goliath.

Envision the scene: Israel's army on one hill and the Philistine army on the other, and between both, in the Valley of Elah, David and Goliath. It is hard to imagine a more unfair contest.

David was a teenage shepherd with no military experience. Goliath was a battle-hardened champion nearly ten feet tall. David's only weapons were a staff and sling. Goliath carried a sword, spear, and javelin. His armor alone weighed more than one hundred pounds. Yet, instead of retreating at the size of Goliath, David raced toward the battle, hurling a single stone as he ran. A moment later, Goliath was dead and headless.

How did David overcome the giant? By understanding that the battle was not his to win but God's. "...the LORD does not save with sword and spear;" he told Goliath, "for the battle is the LORD's." (1 Samuel 17:47)

When we face giant problems, David's battle cry should be ours. For there is always another "Goliath" just over the horizon.

GOLIATH ON THE HORIZON

Goliath approaches.
I hear the thunder of his footsteps punishing the ground,
crushing life, light, and hope.
Boom. Boom. DOOM. Boom.

Dogs whimper. Flowers wither. Rivers run dry.
Birds shriek in cold terror,
lifting off in desperate flight.
Boom. Boom. DOOM. Boom.

I watch numbly, sweating in the fear of Goliath's coming,
looming large, larger,
like a blood-moon waxing on the horizon.
Neckless head.
Blasphemous grin.
Mountainous shoulders.
Granite thighs.
A horrid colossus clad in battle-scarred armor,
in his right hand a weapon,

in his left hand the grave.
Boom. Boom. DOOM. Boom.

He stops, a mountain of flesh blocking the sun.
Close now,
close enough for me to see
the hideous inscriptions on his breastplate:
Fear. Worry. Despair. Disaster. Death.

Slowly, menacingly, the great head turns on steel tendons,
looking north, south, east, west,
fixing last on me.
Me.
I feel the death in those carnivorous, cavernous eyes.

"Bug!" snarls Goliath.
"Come closer, and I will crush you."
He raises his weapon to swat a fly.

"No!" I answer hoarsely.

"No?" he questions, one tree-lined brow arched in surprise.
"You will not come?"

"No," I reply.
"I will not be crushed."

Now the giant bends toward me, eyes full of murder.
"Tell me, rodent," he says,
"who will save you?"

And before I can summon them

23

the words rush to my lips:
"The LORD my God, the LORD of Armies will save me."
The gale of his laughter knocks me to the ground.

"Where is this LORD?" Goliath mocks.
"Where are His armies, weapons, fortresses?"
And once more those carnivorous, cavernous eyes
sweep the landscape, then settle on me.
"Liar!" he hisses.
"You are alone, the servant of a make-believe God."

Face twisted in rage,
he draws himself up to his full height,
higher and higher still,
until the plume of his helmet brushes the clouds
"I am Fear," he thunders.
"I am Worry, Despair, Disaster, Death.
I am Goliath, and I will destroy you!"

As he raises his weapon,
I shout against the clamor:
"You are Fear, but I will not fear you.
You are Worry, but I will not be unnerved.
You are Despair, but I will not lose hope.
You are Disaster, but I will not be harmed.
You are Death, but I will not die.
For this day, the LORD of Armies will strike you down.
My trophy will be your lifeless head."

With trembling fingers
I probe the satchel at my side,
finding at once Goliath's undoing—

the small, smooth stone inscribed with the words
"IT IS WRITTEN."

Loading the Word-stone into my sling,
I run toward the giant;
faster, faster still,
firing the missile blindly in my faith.

And down falls Fear.
Down falls Worry.
Down fall Despair, Disaster, Death.
Down falls Goliath, a dead, conquered monstrosity
vanquished by the Word-stone
unleashed by two trembling hands.

At last the giant, my giant, is dead.

Even so, I will keep the Word-stone of the Almighty
close to my heart,
where I can grasp it the instant
Fear, Worry, Despair, Disaster, or Death appear.

Now I am at peace.
I breathe the sweet air of victory.
But on another day,
on yet another horizon,
another Goliath will appear.
Boom. Boom. DOOM. Boom.

I hear the thunder of his coming.

A Good Night's Sleep

*"I will both lie down in peace, and sleep; for You alone,
O LORD, make me dwell in safety." Psalm 4:8*

At 2:00 A.M. I was still awake, tossing and turning in my bed. I was too worried to sleep. The month before I'd lost my job. Now I had no income, no health insurance, and no way of paying the tower of bills stacked on my microwave. Instead of dreaming, my mind was racing full speed with *what ifs*. What if I get sick? What if I can't pay the monthly lease? What if my car breaks down?

I'd all but given up on sleep, when these words of the psalmist David tiptoed into my consciousness: "I will both lie down in peace, and sleep." The Hebrew word translated as "peace" is *SHALOM*, which also contains the ideas of health, wholeness, happiness, prosperity, safety, and quiet; the very opposite of the restless cover-twisting and mind-racing I'd been doing in bed.

"I will both lie down in peace, and sleep," David wrote. I *will*, not might. Yet, how could he be so confident of a good night's sleep? Were his problems fewer, his worries smaller than ours? No. David wrote Psalm 4 at a time when he was often hungry, thirsty, homeless, and fleeing from the murderous intentions of King Saul. The same Psalm that ends with the promise of peaceful sleep opens with the prayer, "Hear me when I call, O God of my righteousness." (Psalm 4:1)

Though a shepherd, David understood that the means to a good night's sleep was not counting sheep, but counting on the Good Shepherd. "I will both lie down in peace, and sleep," he said, "for You *alone*, O LORD, make me dwell in safety."

There is no sweeter lullaby or faster way to fall sleep than to commit our every problem and burden to the almighty God, who, when watching over us, will neither slumber nor sleep.

A GOOD NIGHT'S SLEEP

Up, down, left, right;
no sleep again tonight.

Bills, health, job, house;
college tuition, unhappy spouse.

Taxes, traffic, sickness, crime;
too much to do, too little time.

Wars, terrorists, Iraq, Iran;
homicide bombers with explosives strapped on.

Climate, oil, wars, coups;
insane dictators, Avian Flu.

Corrupt politicians, national debt;
worry, hurry, stew, and fret.

O rid me, Lord, of this curse,
of trying to control the universe.

Teach me every day anew
to leave my worries up to You.

Remind me that they are Yours to keep,
so I can get a good night's sleep.

Please Have Me Committed

"Where is the wise? Where is the scribe? Where is the disputer of this age? Has not God made foolish the wisdom of this world?" 1 Corinthians 1:20

For decades scholars have searched for a single theory to explain the existence of everything. Many scientists today accept the *Big Bang* theory. According to this hypothesis, the universe and everything in it—space, time, matter, energy, and the physical laws that govern them—came into existence when an infinitesimally small "point of singularity" exploded with unimaginable force.

So far, a uniform theory of everything has eluded scholars. No one can explain what the point of singularity is, where it came from, or why it exploded. No one can explain why the force of gravity is far weaker than the electromagnetic or nuclear force, though each of these forces came from the same source. And yet, scientists admit that if the force of gravity had not been its exact strength, the newly created universe would have collapsed on itself.

I am always amazed when I see such brilliant minds trip over such obvious truths. There is a simple, certain explanation for everything, from the largest galaxies to the smallest, subatomic particles. What is it? What is the true point of singularity? "In the beginning God created the heavens and the earth." (Genesis 1:1)

Of course, the wise and scholarly call this simple belief in the Creator foolishness, and salvation through faith in Jesus Christ insane. But if trusting God is the world's definition of insanity, may we all be "committed" to the certain, eternal, and unyielding truths of God's Word.

PLEASE HAVE ME COMMITTED

Not surprising, Lord.
Not surprising at all that this upside down,
inside out, right side wrong
world of ours consistently, inevitably,
confuses simple with simple-minded.

You invite us to ask.
We receive.

You ask us to seek.
We find.

You urge us to knock,
eagerly waiting to open the door
to a room of bright, immeasurable treasures
the likes of which we could never imagine,
much less ever request.

Yet this same simple hope
the world deems some horrid,
probably contagious,
undoubtedly fatal form of insanity,

foolishly believing it simpler to play God
than to trust in Him.

But I say that if trusting You
for light, life, and salvation,
for every aspect of my life and the lives of those I love—
if this is truly insanity,
then please, Lord, have me committed.

Keep me committed to that one
sane, safe hope:
"Commit your way to the LORD;
trust also in Him, and He shall bring it to pass."

Dream House

"Behold, I stand at the door and knock. If anyone hears
My voice and opens the door, I will come in to him and dine with
him, and he with Me." Revelation 3:20

When I wrote the poem "Dream House," my wife, two sons, and I were living in a new house in Powell, Ohio. It was a beautiful house, the type of house I had always dreamed about: spacious, two stories, fireplace with mantel, oak-paneled doors, two-car garage, quiet neighborhood, and professional landscaping.

Outwardly, we appeared to be a picture-perfect family. My wife and I had good jobs. We owned two cars—one the inevitable minivan for transporting our sons to school, daycare, and soccer matches. And, of course, we had our house, that dream house.

Inwardly, however, the dream was becoming a nightmare. During those same years, our marriage was ripping apart at the seams. Despite counseling, pleading, and tears, I could not reverse or stop the process.

One day, when alone, I began to wander aimlessly through my dream house. As I walked, I felt an overwhelming sense of grief and loneliness. What had gone wrong with my life? Why did I have a house but not a home? How could the house be so beautifully decorated and furnished, yet feel so empty?

It was only then that I realized who and what were missing from the house: the Savior and His Word. In the hectic pursuit of careers and possessions, and amid the daily distractions of life, I had not only neglected to invite Jesus into my dream house; I had actually kicked Him out.

"Behold," He says. "I stand at the door and knock." Which door? Mine. Yours. Everyone's.

KNOCK. KNOCK. KNOCK.
Do you hear Him?

DREAM HOUSE

Lovely house with double stories,
six-panel doors, three lavatories.
Loft, kitchen, unfinished basement,
upscale neighborhood—
now that makes a statement.

Grass is green. Yard looks great.
Flowers are blooming. Edging is straight.
Trees are so tall, laden with seeds.
Sculpted mulch, no sign of weeds.

Pretty house, a lifelong dream;
yet, not so perfect as it outwardly seems.
Despite the garage and hardwood mantel,
the low-rate mortgage and equity potential,
the rooms feel cold, the walls look bare,

the air smells old because Christ is not there—
not like He was at the very start,
in my home, tasks, relationships, and heart.

Now in times of sorrow and despair,
when I wander through rooms,
wondering why He's not there;
when I raise my fists heavenward and begin to shout,
I remember: Christ did not leave.
I kicked Him out.

Place of the Skull

"And He, bearing His cross, went out to a place called the Place of a Skull, which is called in Hebrew, Golgotha." John 19:17

The exact location of Golgotha is uncertain. We do know that it was outside the city gates of Jerusalem, close enough to a road for travelers to ridicule the crucified Jesus, and also near a garden and the unused tomb of Joseph from Arimathea.

Ultimately, however, the location of Golgotha is not important. What is important is that Jesus Christ, God the Son, was crucified there to atone for the sins of the world. In the truest sense, Golgotha stands at the "cross-road" of history. Every Old Testament promise of redemption anticipated it. Every New Testament book heralds it as the fulfillment of God's plan to redeem the world.

The message of the cross is the message of the Gospel. The apostle Paul wrote in 1 Corinthians 1:23-24, "...but we preach Christ crucified, to the Jews a stumbling block and to the Greeks foolishness, but to those who are called, both Jews and Greeks, Christ the power of God and the wisdom of God."

Golgotha is also the cross-road of our individual lives: the power and wisdom of God by which we conduct ourselves, make choices, and determine priorities. Christ "died for all," wrote Paul, "that those who live should live no longer for themselves, but for Him who died for them and rose again." (2 Corinthians 5:15)

Can we truly stand at Golgotha, see the Savior bleeding and dying for us, and not be changed?

PLACE OF THE SKULL

In the gloom of this black day
I leave the excited uproar of the city
and walk toward the dreaded Place of the Skull.

On a sign, a disjointed skeletal finger points the way:
"This way to the Place of the Skull," it mocks.
"Join the fun.
Bring the family.
Watch the Christ suffer."

Two boys brush hurriedly past,
sandals loose and robes flapping.
"Out'ta my way," says one.
"Yeah," says the other. "Out'ta the way.
We wanna see the nailing."
They disappear into the gloom,
swallowed by the lust to see God die.

I follow, feeling more dread and terror
with each halting step.
Before me the path to Golgotha, Place of the Skull,
winds through the Friday gloom
like an angry white cut.
In the harsh soil I can clearly see
the furrow of the heavy cross,

drops of blood,
the place where You,
dear Lord of heaven and earth,
stumbled, fell, and stood again,
willing Yourself to go on.

There is another sign.
It reads, "King of the Jews a quarter mile ahead."
And still another, "Food, drinks, souvenirs."
And after that, "Have your photo taken with the Son of
God."

How did You walk this path, Lord;
how, why, for a creation that repaid Your love
and benevolence with willful disobedience
and an all-too-eager appetite to watch You die?

Suddenly, I see it,
the stony precipice of Golgotha:
eyeless sockets, tombstone teeth, lichen brows,
bone-littered scalp hosting three crosses—
Yours in the middle,
Yours the only cross that matters.

Here, at the Place of the Skull,
the very air reeks of blood, pain, and death.
The noises chill my spine and rend my soul:
hammering, screaming, pleading,
the coarse laughter of Roman soldiers
who pound the nails with glee,
snickering at punch-lines about whores and thieves
and a silly Jewish rabbi, who believed Himself

37

to be the Son of God.
Ha! Ha! Ha!

They don't know;
they can't see in Your crucified body
God's own arms open wide to embrace the sinful world,
to embrace even them.

I watch. I listen. I weep,
knowing that I am as guilty as they are;
as guilty of bringing You, Lord Jesus,
to this Place of the Skull;
as guilty as the high priest who condemned You;
as guilty as Pilate who washed his hands of You.

That You, Lord, should allow Yourself to die here
at the Place of the Skull
is far beyond my comprehension
and farther beyond my merit.
I deserve nothing, absolutely nothing,
except the stony grin of that Skull itself.

O misery of all miseries.
O mystery of all mysteries.
At the Place of the Skull,
God hangs on a tree;
the Alpha and the Omega,
the Beginning and the End;
the Almighty One who cast galaxies
across the infinite expanse of space
and gave us, His most prized possessions,
a universe to enjoy and explore.

Lord God, Savior of my life,
how can I leave this Place of the Skull
unmoved by Your love,
ungrateful for Your sacrifice?

How can I watch You bleed and die,
yet live only for myself?
How can I watch You reconcile the world to God,
yet claim that I have irreconcilable differences—
no reason to live, love, or forgive?

I can't, Lord;
not if I've truly been to the Place of the Skull;
not if I've seen You looking down on me
in bleeding grace;
looking down on me.

On me.

Me.

In God's Gymnasium

"For when I am weak, then I am strong." 2 Corinthians 12:10

Our English word *gymnasium* is derived from the Greek word *GYMNOS*, which means "naked." Ancient Greek athletes trained and competed in the nude. The rationale for this practice was that clothing hindered competition.

Ancient gymnasiums did not have Nautilus machines or electric-powered treadmills, but they were equipped with ropes for climbing, tracks for running, animal-skin bags for punching, and weights for lifting. Calisthenics were often done to music, an ancient form of Jazzercise.

People have been going to the gym for millennia. While the design and equipment have changed, the purpose of going has not. We go to the gym to sweat and work out, to improve strength and stamina, and to lose weight and build muscle.

God has a gymnasium too. It is not a place, but a means by which He strips us bare—*GYMNOS*, naked—of self-righteousness and wrong living, destructive pride and earthly excess; and builds up our spiritual muscle by exercising our faith. This exercise often takes the form of *weights* and *waits*; that is, heavy burdens and long-suffering. Workouts like these are seldom pleasant, but they are necessary for our spiritual growth and well-being.

Our physical muscles actually grow bigger and stronger when they are "torn down" through exercise. Faith grows bigger and stronger when God tears down our notions of personal strength and clearly shows us our human weaknesses.

In God's gymnasium, faith gets the workout.

IN GOD'S GYMNASIUM

I'm back again
in God's gymnasium.

I'd never come here on my own.
I prefer home
and the comfort of my couch,
where I can be a spiritual slouch,
growing fat and fatter
on Things That Don't Matter.

Here the weights are heavy.
Just ask me:
divorces, failures, depression, ills,
frets, regrets, joblessness, bills.
I sweat and struggle, and when I'm done
I've not been able to budge even one.

Yet, by these weights I learn at length
that in my weakness God shows His strength.
When He delays and seems to tarry,

He is teaching me to let Him carry
my burdens and sorrows,
my todays and tomorrows.

Why am I always so surprised
that faith itself needs exercise,
if it is to grow and stay strong
and keep on keeping on?

Amid the sweat of problems and stress,
God strips away self-righteousness.
He teaches me what's right and meet
so I can be His athlete;
winning the prize and the end of the race
by running each step in His amazing grace.

This I'm here to learn again;
here in God's gymnasium.

Jesus, a Sight for Sore Eyes

"One thing I know: that though I was blind, now I see!" John 9:25

He was a beggar, blind from birth. He had never seen his parents, or the magnificent temple in Jerusalem, or the brilliant colors of a sunset. Unable to work, he spent his days begging, hoping to hear the clink of coins tossed into a cup.

Then one day, Jesus found the blind beggar and worked miracles in his life. The first miracle was restored sight. We can only imagine how the once-blind beggar must have wept and danced for joy, shouting, "I can see! I can see!"

Yet, that same day Jesus worked an even greater miracle in this man's life; namely, the miracle of faith; the miracle of seeing Jesus as He truly is, the Son of God and Savior of the world—something no mortal can see apart from the Holy Spirit.

However, when the once-blind beggar looked at Jesus with his restored sight and newly opened eyes of faith, he did see the long-promised Redeemer. "Do you believe in the Son of God?" asked Jesus. And the man replied, "Lord, I believe!" (John 9:35, 38)

"One thing I know: that though I was blind, now I see!" Each of us can say this with the once-blind beggar, because the same miracle of faith has been worked in our lives. God the Holy Spirit has opened our eyes to see Jesus Christ as our Lord and Savior. And oh, how different the world looks because of Him!

In Scripture, believing is seeing.

JESUS, A SIGHT FOR SORE EYES

Jesus, my eyes are sore.
I've been crying.

I've looked and looked,
but I can't see You
or the fulfillment of Your promise
to answer my prayers,
ease my burdens,
and lift me up to the realms of eagles,
where I can soar unfettered on wings of grace.

Where are You, Lord?
Why are You hiding?
Why do You cloak Yourself in an impenetrable
cloud of silence and mystery?

Do You see me?

I've searched for You.
I've looked everywhere.
Day after day, I've stood here
shielding my eyes against the heat and sun,
straining to see You or some sign of Your coming;

some token, no matter how light or trivial,
that You even care.

But all I see is me—
my sins, my problems,
the frustration and despair that sweep over me
like snarling, swelling breakers,
dragging me grain by pitiful grain
into a deep, unforgiving sea of sorrow.

O God, I don't like what I see.

Sometimes, I just want to close my eyes
and make the world go away,
but it won't—not even for a moment.

I'm like that poor, blind beggar,
fumbling, stumbling, groping,
with no other means to judge my worth
than the hollow, metallic clink of coins
tossed into a cup.
Coins!

Until I feel Your touch
(is it You, Lord?),
and hear Your words
(it is You, Lord!),
and learn again what I swore I'd never forget.

I've searched for You in all the wrong places.
I've crawled at last to the place
I should have run first—Your Word.

The Word that opens sore,
beggarly eyes like mine
to see in You the love, worth, and deliverance
I've been too blind to see;
the omnipotent arms outstretched to hold me;
the immeasurable love that stooped down to save me;
the priceless blood poured out to cleanse me;
the healing words, waiting, ever working
to open my sore eyes to a World Other Than This One,
to the God Who takes in what society casts out.

Instead of fumbling, groping,
and counting the coins in my tin cup,
I should have been listening to You:
"Do you believe in the Son of God?"
Because before I can see, I must believe.

I believe, Lord.
Now I see.

The Homecoming

"But when he was still a great way off, his father saw him and had compassion, and ran and fell on his neck and kissed him." Luke 15:20

The Parable of the Prodigal Son is one of my favorites. Part of the reason lies in my love of homecomings. When only fifteen, I left my home in Florida to attend Immanuel Lutheran High School in Eau Claire, Wisconsin. Almost imperceptibly, high school became college; college, seminary; and seminary, ministry—which led to many other changes in my life. For more than four decades my life was a series of homecomings, each more anticipated and treasured than the last.

An even greater reason for my appreciation of the prodigal son is that I have been one, too often running away from my heavenly Father, forgetting even to wave goodbye, pursuing foolish ambitions or desires that inevitably led me to the same pigpen and empty husks. And yet, each time I came to my senses—a beautiful description of repentance—the heavenly Father welcomed me home with wide open arms.

It is the image of the father in the parable that comforts me most. When we look at our lives and misdeeds, we often wonder how God could possibly forgive us or welcome us home. But in this parable, told by God the Son Himself, we have our answer.

Whenever we come to our senses and return to God in repentance, He always welcomes us home. Not only does He welcome us, but He runs to meet us. He embraces us despite the pig-stink on our clothing. He celebrates our return.

How comforting to know that when we do run away, the Father's love goes with us. And it is the Father's love that brings us safely home.

THE HOMECOMING

So many times I've run away, saying,
"Father, I'll be right back."
Then I was gone for months, even years,
never knowing where I was at;
never knowing where I was going
or what I planned to do;
but in my youthful arrogance believing
that alone was better than home with You.

Down the stairs and out the door,
nearly slipping in my haste,
places to go, people to see,
a Father's inheritance to waste.

And waste it I did
on lusts, husks, and whores,
who took away my everything
and then demanded even more.

When I had no more to give,
no friends to call, no place to live,
no food to eat, no water to drink,
I lay down with the other pigs
and wallowed in the stink.

I shivered in the cold.
I blistered in the sun.
And when I grew desperate enough,
I ate kernels mixed with dung.

In that desperation, Father,
I suddenly thought of You.
I came to all my senses
and realized what I must do.
Home.
I must go home
to the Father's love I'd always known.

That day I left the pigpen,
reeking of dung, followed by flies,
walking the road with disgusted travelers
who quickly stepped aside.

"Who could love a wretch like that?" they asked.
"Who could welcome him?"
He's soiled and sick.
He's gaunt and stinks.
He's paying the wages of sin."
And after what I'd done, where I'd been,
I knew they were right.

Through the long days and nights
I walked on, my head low with shame,
wondering with every step, Father,
if You might feel the same.

Why would You love a wretch like me?
Why would You welcome me home,
when I'd squandered my inheritance
and set out on my own;
when I'd worried You so by leaving
and ignored all Your advice,
and turned to see You waving goodbye
with tears glinting in Your eyes.

The last mile home was the hardest.
My stomach roiled. My knees felt slack.
At the final bend in that too-familiar road
I stopped, turned, looked back.

It was then I heard You calling, Father.
I've never forgotten what You said:
"My son has returned home to Me,
alive, though he was dead."

You took me into Your gracious arms,
ignoring the stench and flies,
forgiving the unforgivable,
and above all making me realize
that no matter how long I'd been away,
no matter where I'd roamed,
Your redemptive love had followed me there
to bring me all the way back home.

Stop Crying, Start Living

"When the Lord saw her, He had compassion on her
and said to her, 'Do not weep.'" Luke 7:13

After healing the centurion's servant in Capernaum, Jesus and the crowd following Him walked the twenty-five miles to the small town of Nain. As they approached the town gate, they met another crowd leaving the city—this one a funeral procession.

How different the crowds were! Leading the one crowd was Jesus, whom Scripture calls the "Resurrection" and the "Life." At the front of the other crowd, carried in a coffin, was a dead man—young, the only son of his widowed mother. Not only had his death left her completely alone and heartbroken, but also without any means of financial support.

When the Lord saw the woman, "He had compassion on her." Contemplate the magnitude of this simple statement. When the *Lord* saw her—the Lord, the Creator of heaven and earth, the God we so often accuse of being distant and uncaring.

And what did Jesus say to the woman? "Do not weep." Then, touching the coffin, Jesus said to the dead man, "Young man, I say to you, arise." And to the amazement of the crowds, the young man sat up and began to speak.

When we are tempted to doubt the importance and power of God's Word in our lives, let us remember Nain. For with one and the same Word, Jesus dried a widow's tears and raised her dead son to life. It is the same Word of the same Lord that empowers us to stop crying and start living.

STOP CRYING, START LIVING

Nain:
dwelling of nameless, faceless people
lost in small-town insignificance,
with no claim to notoriety or cause for mention
save a widow's grief and the Savior's compassion.

Dialogue:
mostly weeping;
gasps of black misery seeping to the surface
from the coldest, darkest recesses of the human soul.

Script:
from tragedy to triumph.
Two processions of no similarity
converging on Nain City Limits—
Jesus, Life-Giver, leading the one;
Death, Man-Killer, leading the other.

Tension, silence, as the two companies meet,
their battle-line clearly drawn
in pale, cemetery soil.
But which shall give way: Life or Death?

With tenderness immeasurable
the Lord of All steps to the nameless widow.
He aches for her, with her;
such sadness, so alone;
her small frame bent by sorrow;
tears welling from swollen, red eyes
fed by sour springs of human misery.

In the blackness of that hour
she knows not that the God she thought
blind and deaf,
so heartlessly capricious in His power,
now stands only inches from her need.
Inches.

Softly, tenderly, He speaks to her:
"Stop crying!"
And though countless mourners in dark days past
have voiced similar words
(theirs so hollow and impotent),
His words penetrate to the core of her anguish,
bringing sudden, glad resurrection
to a hope more dead than her son.

Hope:
to feel alive again;
to rejoice.

Like frost before the morning sun
her tears melt in the warmth of Christ's presence.
In startled expectation she watches the Life-Giver
step to the coffin of her dead son and speak again—

speak what no mourner of Adam's empty heritage
would dare speak: "Start living!"

And in that sacred instant,
as the living, breathing words strike dead, deaf ears,
the corpse rises,
blinking in Nain's bright sunlight,
marveling at his coffin-bed
and the rippling gasps of black-clad mourners.

Hot tears course down the widow's cheeks,
fed this time by sweet springs of joy.
She runs to the coffin,
nearly tripping in her ecstasy,
and there embraces her resurrected son.

The reunion complete,
she turns trembling to face her Benefactor
and finds Him smiling.
Smiling!
A wondrously radiant smile
that would set kingdoms to laughing
if seen in its fullness.

She tries to speak,
but there are no words large or holy enough
to convey her gratitude.
Yet, somehow, the Life-Giver knows this too.

Gently dismissing her thanks
with a wave of His divine hand,
He speaks to the widow once more:

"My gift to you," says the Life-Giver.
"I give you back your son."

The world is Nain,
insignificant dwelling where
nameless, faceless people
march solemnly, constantly, irreversibly
toward a common cemetery;
their leader, Death;
their music, a dirge;
in their caskets their dreams and hopes,
aspirations and accomplishments.

O Sovereign Lord,
how, when, where does this death-march end?
Strangely, it ends in a cemetery;
not yours, not mine,
not even the cold, pale soil
outside of Nain City Limits.

It ends in that once-used sepulcher
outside of Old Jerusalem, where Jesus Christ,
World-Maker, Sin-Bearer, Life-Giver,
was dead, buried, and resurrected.

"Widow, stop crying!
Corpse, start living!"
Words of the Life-Giver,
doing for the one what they did to the other.

Come to Nain, where it is ever heard:
"Life, not Death, spoke the final word."

Wretch that I Am

*"O wretched man that I am! Who will deliver me
from this body of death? I thank God—through Jesus Christ
our Lord!" Romans 7:24-25*

Wretched man? Body of death? What would make the apostle Paul say such things? He actually tells us several times in Romans 7, typified by such statements as "For the good that I will to do, I do not do; but the evil I will not to do, that I practice." (Romans 7:19)

It was this ongoing struggle that led Paul to cry out, "O wretched man that I am!" Even the Greek word translated as "wretched" is instructive. It literally means to have a callus. How does one get a callus? By doing the same painfully hard work over and over. For a Christian, what can be more painful than having the desire to do good, yet succumbing to evil?

I want to be a good parent, but fail. I want to trust God more, but find myself doubting His willingness to help. I want to glorify God, but find myself drawn to lusting or coveting or even taking the holy name of God in vain. The list is endless. The result is wretchedness.

The difficulty with living the new life in Christ is our old sinful nature. As Christians, we are not controlled by the old nature; we are led by the Holy Spirit. Yet, our old nature still makes itself known, warring against all that is good and godly.

When we assess our lives honestly, we too must cry out with the apostle Paul, "O wretched man that I am! Who will deliver me from this body of death?" And with Paul we praise God for the answer: "Jesus Christ our Lord."

Jesus, who loves and forgives a wretch like me.

WRETCH THAT I AM

My mind is in the gutter,
when it should be on things above.
I'm far too quick to anger,
and far too slow to love.

Instead of giving thanks
for all the blessings I receive,
I steal away to spend them
like an ordinary thief.

Fearful is my first name,
Ingrate is my last.
I'm fearful of the future
and ungrateful for the past.

At the Altar of Worldly Pleasure
I prostrate myself like a whore.
I view God's unlimited forgiveness
as a license to sin even more.

Rather than staying close to God

or yearning to hear His Word,
I yearn to recall the punch-line
of a filthy joke I heard.

I wander off the narrow path.
I keep bad company.
With one mouth I speak blessings and curses.
Dear Lord, how can this be?

I'm like a lamp beneath a bowl
and salt with little flavor.
The only time I turn to God
is when I need a favor.

Oh, what a wretched man I am
with sinful nature as my lot;
failing to do the good I should,
doing the evil I should not.

Who will rescue me from this body of death?
Who will set me free?
Thanks be to God in heaven above!
In Christ He gives me victory!

When I fall, He picks me up
and bids me only trust.
He takes me by the hand and leads.
He knows I'm only dust.

He forgives me my countless sins
with grace that defies all measure.
Then He works in me to will and do

according to His good pleasure.

Of all the things I wonder about,
this is the greatest mystery:
that even God should have such grace
to love a wretch like me.

The Seven Words

"And when they had mocked Him, they took the robe off Him, put His own clothes on Him, and led Him away to be crucified." Matthew 27:31

The Passion of our Savior is recorded in all four Gospels. The composite picture is enough to rend our hearts. Yet, Scripture relates the events of Maundy Thursday and Good Friday in a relatively "bloodless" way. For example, the Gospel of John describes the flogging of Jesus in one sentence: "So then Pilate took Jesus and scourged Him." (John 19:1) It says nothing about the type of whip used or the number of lashes received.

The same reserved description is given of Christ's crucifixion: They "led Him away to be crucified." Yet, we know from both ancient historians and modern archaeological discoveries how gruesome death by crucifixion was.

Reserved for the vilest or most dangerous of criminals, crucifixion was designed to maximize shame and pain and prolong agony. Death could take days.

Iron spikes were often used to nail the condemned to the cross. Due to the position of the body, the cause of death was frequently suffocation. Inhaling was difficult. Exhaling was all but impossible without putting weight on the legs, which were usually bent, sometimes broken, and supported only by the spikes driven through the heels.

Under these circumstances, we can only imagine how difficult it must have been for Jesus to speak. But according to the Gospels, Jesus did speak seven times while hanging on the cross—not curses or desperate pleas for mercy, but words of forgiveness, love, compassion, and victory.

Despite the struggle to breathe, these words of Jesus were spoken in a loud, clear voice: "It is finished!"

THE SEVEN WORDS

Maundy Thursday,
the twilight between two Covenants.
As the night darkens,
God's promised Day dawns.

"I have eagerly desired to eat this Passover with you
before I suffer."
There is urgency in the Master's voice.
Then the hands that once shaped stars
break the bread and bless the cup.

There is talk of betrayal.
"Surely not I?" ask the Twelve, one by one.
But before the night is ended,
they will all learn the lesson of "grace alone";
for they will all forsake Him and flee.

Midnight. Gethsemane.

The very air is thick with death and sorrow.
Jesus sweats.
He sweats blood,
for the Lord God has laid on Him
the iniquity of us all.

Friday, called "Good."
God on trial, as He still is by the worldly wise and
arrogant.
"Tell us plainly!" demands Caiaphas,
his face red with rage and pomposity.
"Tell us if You are the Christ!"

"Yes," Jesus tells them plainly;
and they condemn Him to die.

He stands before Pilate.
The Roman procurator wants nothing to do
with this righteous Man,
and so, like all the world, becomes
guilty of complicity.

Outside the Hall of Man's Justice
a mob incites to riot.
"Look at this man!" shouts Pilate.
"Look at this man, if not the evidence!
Is He worth your time or the cost of the nails?"

"Give us Barabbas! Kill Jesus!"
the mob answers in gleeful unison.
It is the only "decision for Christ"
natural man can make.

Nails. Blows. Blood. Pain.
God's love incarnate is lifted high for the blind to see.
And it is love, not rusty Roman nails,
that keeps Christ there.

Listen! He speaks:
**"Father, forgive them,
for they do not know what they are doing."**

Not forgive if desirable.
Not forgive if possible.
Christ's blood is the imperative:
"Father, forgive!"
Forgive the priests and soldiers.
Forgive the mob and world.

And the Father answers,
"Forgiven! Forever!
Tell them to call Me Father."

He speaks again:
**"I tell you the truth,
today you will be with Me in paradise."**

"With Me."
So near is the Crucified One to our human misery.
"Paradise."
So rich is the prospect of His presence.
"Today."
So immediate and complete is the healing in His wounds.

He speaks a third time:

"Dear woman, here is your son."
And to the disciple with her,
"Here is your mother."

There is a tenderness here.
Mothers know.
As Mary hears His words,
she hears others spoken long before:
"A sword will pierce your own soul, too."

She feels that piercing grief.
She aches for her Son and Savior.
She remembers holding His little hands
to steady His first steps.
Now His hands are nailed to the cross.
She recalls the warmth of His embrace.
Now His arms are spread wide to embrace the world.

"Do you not know that I must be about
My Father's business?"
His words had puzzled her when spoken.
Now, standing beneath the cross,
she puzzles even more as the Father's business
reaches its appointed end.

He speaks a fourth time:
"Eloi, Eloi, lama sabachthani?
My God, My God,
why have You forsaken Me?"

It is the cry of the damned.
It is the black horror of sin.

It is a cry of incomparable misery and mystery.
It is absolute darkness,
so that even heaven and earth turn from the sight
of God dying on an accursed tree.

He speaks a fifth time:
"I am thirsty."

His thirst is our thirst;
the thirst for rest, purpose, and belonging;
the thirst for something lasting and eternal;
the thirst for something outside of ourselves
and the smallness of our dreams;
the thirst for something of which time cannot rob us
and death cannot cheat us.

Thirst.
Thirst for the living God.
Thirst quenched in the One who proclaimed:
"If a man is thirsty, let him come to Me and drink.
Whoever believes in Me, as the Scripture has said,
streams of living water will flow from within him."

He speaks a sixth time:
"It is finished."

The crowd said, "It's over."
The soldiers said, "It's done."
The priests said, "He's finished."
The disciples took His lifeless body down from the tree.

And yet, in God's redemptive plan,

when all seemed lost,
precisely then all were won.
"It is finished."
This was Christ's cry of victory,
in perpetuity,
of an irrevocably complete salvation.

In that instant,
over our lives of incomplete efforts
and outstanding debits
God wrote "Finished!"
in the priceless blood of His own Son.

In that instant,
when the books were closed
and the verdict was rendered,
our guilt was removed from us farther
than east is from west.

With His own two hands,
God planted the cross of Jesus Christ
so firmly in this redeemed world
that the earth shook, boulders split, graves opened.

And out of the ruins there rose a joyful new song:
"The kingdom of the world has become
the kingdom of our Lord and of His Christ,
and He will reign forever and ever."

He speaks a final time:
**"Father, into Your hands
I commit My spirit."**

From "Father, forgive!" to "Father, I commit!"
All for you,
and for you all.

He speaks. Do you hear Him?

Waiting

"I wait for the LORD, my soul waits,
and in His Word I do hope." Psalm 130:5

Even in the best of times, waiting for the Lord to act or answer can be difficult. But when we are in deep trouble, as was the writer of Psalm 130—"out of the depths I have cried to You, O LORD," he said—waiting can seem impossible. Long days and sleepless nights easily become the fertile soil for seeds of doubt: "Where is God? If He cared about me, would He make me wait?"

Yet, amid his troubles and fears, the psalmist insisted, "I wait for the LORD, my soul waits." The Hebrew word he used, like many Bible words for waiting, contains the idea of strength and patience.

The psalmist was willing to wait for the Lord, because he fully expected the Lord to deliver him; the same hopeful expectation in which watchmen wait for the first gray sliver of dawn and the new day certain to follow. It was this confident hope that enabled the psalmist to go on waiting for the Lord.

But where does such hope originate? The psalmist tells us this too. His ability to wait for the Lord came from the same infallible power source that you and I have in our homes and hearts: the Word of God. "In His Word I do hope," wrote the psalmist. The only Word on earth that will never disappoint us or fail to deliver what it promises.

God does not make us wait because He's indifferent, uncaring, or too busy governing the universe; rather, because He's loving, caring, and irrevocably committed to our daily and eternal well-being. To know and believe this is to find the strength to wait for God to act in His own time and way.

Just wait. You'll see.

WAITING

"Wait," says the Lord.
But that is so hard to do
when there is no job in sight
and the bills are all due;

when the car needs repair,
a marriage is failing,
depression sets in,
body is ailing;

when life lacks purpose
and friends don't call,
misery rises,
hopes fall;

when loved ones are sick
and it's impossible to rest,
while waiting for results
of some medical test;

when each day looks the same
and each night is too long,
and there seems no way
to keep on keeping on;

when I look at my problems,
but don't see God there,
and assume that to mean
that God does not care.

For if God did care,
why would He wait,
knowing that waiting
is something I hate?

Oh, forgive me, Lord,
for my arrogance,
my ingratitude, poor attitude,
and self-righteousness.

For in the very act of waiting
You want me to see
that waiting for You
is good for me.

Though difficult and unwanted,
painful and long,
waiting builds up my faith
and makes me strong.

It gives me character,
perseverance, and hope.

It teaches me to conquer
instead of just cope.

It frees me from the smallness
of instant gratification,
forcing me to focus
on Your lasting salvation.

It reminds me that waiting
is ordained by Your love,
so that the gifts I wait for
are gifts from above.

So, I will wait for You, Lord,
I will call on Your name,
knowing that waiting for You
is never waiting in vain.

When Hope Lies Dead and Buried

*"Now Jesus loved Martha and her sister and Lazarus.
So, when He heard that he was sick, He stayed
two more days in the place where He was." John 11:5-6*

When Lazarus became ill, Mary and Martha sent word to Jesus, saying, "Lord, behold, he whom You love is sick." (John 11:3) Yet, instead of leaving immediately, Jesus remained where He was for two days. How could Jesus love Lazarus and still delay going to him?

The answer lies first in understanding the nature of God's love. The Greek word used in John 11:5 for love is *AGAPE*; and *AGAPE* is the love of deep understanding and committed purpose. This is the same word used in John 3:16, "For God so loved the world that He gave His only begotten Son."

As strange or troubling as it may seem, Jesus delayed going to Lazarus because He loved him. According to John 11:5-6, "Now Jesus loved Martha and her sister and Lazarus. *So*, when He heard that he was sick, He stayed two more days in the place where He was."

It was because of His love that Jesus delayed going to Bethany. He wanted Mary and Martha to see Him as the Resurrection and the Life. This they did when they stood before the tomb of dead and buried Lazarus, and heard Jesus command in a loud voice, "Lazarus, come forth!" (John 11:43)

"Did I not say to you that if you would believe you would see the glory of God?" Jesus said to Martha. (John 11:40) When our hopes lie dead and buried, He says the same to us. In His great, purposeful love for us, God may delay in our lives. But as the resurrection of Lazarus teaches, God can never arrive too late.

WHEN HOPE LIES DEAD AND BURIED

I followed Christ to Bethany,
though the journey seemed senseless to me
now that Lazarus was dead.

"I'll go," I said to the Lord,
"but I can ill afford
to waste my time on lost causes."

"Maybe it isn't my place to speak,
but shouldn't we have gone to Bethany last week,
when Lazarus was still alive?"

However, the Savior did not say
one word about His delay
other than "This is for God's glory."

So, I followed Christ to Bethany,
dreading "the talk" with family:
"Martha, Mary, I am so sorry for your loss."

Multitudes came that day to mourn,

dressed in black, faces forlorn.
Jesus wept, too.

Mary and Martha approached Jesus at different times,
but with an identical concern on their minds:
"If You had been here, my brother would not have died."

"Your brother Lazarus will rise from his grave."
"Yes," replied Martha, "on the Last Day."
Jesus said, "I am the Resurrection and the Life."

What that meant I didn't know.
I just wanted to go
someplace, any place, other than a cemetery.

Martha led to where Lazarus was laid.
Reluctantly, I joined the parade
of people who'd come to pay final respects.

"Roll away the stone," Jesus said.
"No, Lord," Martha pleaded. "He's four days dead.
The odor will be unbearable."

Jesus looked at Martha and then at me.
"Don't doubt," He said. "Just believe
and you will see the glory of God."

I heard it then, a single loud shout:
"Lazarus!" cried Jesus. "Come out!
Come out of your grave!"

And out Lazarus came,

still wearing the same
linens and spices in which he'd been buried.

At this I fell to my knees
and begged Christ, "Please!
Please forgive my pride and arrogance!"

This is why You said to me,
"Follow Me to Bethany."
You wanted me to see the glory of God.

The truth is, from the first day I went
I've considered my time well spent
at the tomb of Lazarus.

For in Bethany I learned to carry
hopes long dead and buried
to the living Christ.

Gone Fishing

"'Cast the net on the right side of the boat, and you will find some.' So they cast, and now they were not able to draw it in because of the multitude of fish." John 21:6

After His resurrection, Jesus appeared to His disciples over forty days, showing Himself to be alive by many infallible proofs. None of these appearances were accidental. Jesus chose the times and places to teach His disciples specific lessons. But what lessons could be learned in an ordinary setting like fishing?

In a sense, the ordinariness of the setting was the lesson. Jesus wanted His disciples to understand that His resurrection was meant not only for Easter Day, but for the days after Easter; not only for a walk to Emmaus, but for a fishing trip on Lake Galilee.

The disciples were professional fishermen. Yet, on their own, they caught nothing. However, when they heard and heeded the words of Jesus, "Cast the net on the right side of the boat, and you will find some," they caught an abundance of fish.

Are you "fishing" for something in life: peace, purpose, the certainty of salvation? You won't find these things fishing alone. You will find them in Jesus Christ and His Word. If this sounds too simple—isn't that a good thing?

"Cast the net on the right side of the boat" may have sounded simple, even silly, to the disciples after a long, fishless night. But the Word of God proved to be the answer they needed.

God's Word has the answers we need. It really is that simple and comforting. The Word of God always directs us to the "right side" of the boat.

GONE FISHING

"I'm bored."
"Me too."
"What should we do?"
"I don't know."
"Peter, do you?"
"Let's go fishing," Peter said.

So we went and spent
hours on the lake.
Such a mistake.
By the time we were done
we'd failed to catch one.
Not one fish.

"Try here."
"No, try there."
The truth is, we tried everywhere.
Each of us thought
our favorite spot

would be teeming with fish.

And as the night wore on,
we grew tired and irritable.
One by one we began to quibble.
"Now what should we do?"
"I don't know. Do you?"
"Let's go home," Peter said.

Weighing anchor,
raising the net,
we sailed for home trying to forget
that fishless night.
Finally, with dawn and shore in sight,
we saw Him.

A Man in the distance.
And next to the Man was a small breakfast fire.
Waving one arm, He began to inquire:
"Have you caught any fish?"
Peter answered for us all, "We wish.
But no. Not one."

Then the strangest thing happened.
The Man replied in a familiar voice
that made us inexplicably want to rejoice,
"Stow away your fisherman's pride.
If you want to catch fish, cast the net on the right side
of the boat."

So, we did.
And why we did, I can't say—

except that there was power in the way
He had spoken from a distance,
power that overcame our know-it-all resistance
and replaced it with trust.

One more cast of the net.
Just one.
And when we were done
the number of fish we caught was so great
that our fishing net began to break.
Praise God!

"It is the Lord!"
I heard Peter shout.
Removing his coat, he dove out
of the boat, swimming faster and faster
toward the One he recognized as Lord and Master,
the risen Jesus Christ.

Dear, brash Simon Peter.
None of us did what Peter had dared.
Yet, when we finally arrived we found breakfast prepared.
United by faith we stood silently on shore,
warmed by fire and the God we adored.
Praise the Lord!

Yes, praise the risen, victorious Lord,
who over a period of forty days
appeared to us in a variety of ways;
on the road to Emmaus, in the locked upper room,
in the brightness of Easter and the darkness of gloom.
But always for a reason. Always.

That fishless night had a reason too.
Jesus appeared to us in that practical setting
to teach us a lesson, and to keep us from forgetting
that while a fisherman learns a lot of stuff,
a fisherman's skills are not always enough
to catch fish.

And in a way, we're all like fishermen.
We may not fish on Lake Galilee,
but we do fish our way through humanity,
casting our net here and there,
looking for salvation everywhere.
But it can be found only in Christ.

So I keep a plaque on one wall at home.
It reads, "If you want to catch fish, take Christ along."
I've given this matter a lot of thought
now that the Word of God is my favorite fishing spot.
See you there.
Soon, I hope.

House Plan

"For every house is built by someone,
but He who built all things is God." Hebrews 3:4

Creation is a matter of faith; a matter of taking God at His Word. The first sentence of the Bible tells us, "In the beginning God created the heavens and the earth." (Genesis 1:1) And the writer of Hebrews reminds us, "By faith we understand that the worlds were framed by the word of God, so that the things which are seen were not made of things which are visible." (Hebrews 11:3)

In academia evolution is presented as "scientific" and creationism as superstition. But the reality is that evolution requires its own kind of faith, because evolution is not provable. It's a theory, and not a very good one at that. It not only violates principles of the so-called Scientific Method—to be valid a theory must be observable and repeatable—it's also contrary to common sense.

Common sense tells us that a building has a builder. "For every house is built by someone," said the writer of Hebrews. Would any one of us, including any rational evolutionist, look at a house and say, "That house built itself?" No. Give it a billion years. Give it a trillion years. Buy all the building materials and place them neatly on a vacant piece of property. But that house will never build itself.

Accepting that God created the world in six ordinary days by speaking it into existence will always require faith—the type of faith worked by the Holy Spirit. Yet, God has also left evidence in creation itself that should lead every human being to acknowledge Him as the Creator and to seek to learn more about Him.

HOUSE PLAN

Can a house build itself,
devise its own plan,
purchase its property,
landscape its land?

Can it lay its foundation,
raise its own walls,
attach its own roof,
carve out its halls?

Can it install its own power,
its windows and doors,
its plumbing and lighting,
its ceilings and floors?

Can it finance its mortgage,
and when this is over,
find the right family
to be its new owner?

The answer is "no"—
that's plain to see.
A house building itself

is, well, just silly.

And if this notion is silly,
is it not far worse
to assume the same
of the universe?

The universe displays
intelligent design,
not random accidents
over eons of time.

Sun and moon,
stars and earth,
from the vastness of space
to the miracle of birth;

plants and animals,
land and weather,
everything God made
works together.

Just open your heart
and you will see:
God built the universe
with His "Let there be!"

The only alternative
needs a lot of help—
that a house can somehow
build itself.

Slow to Believe

"O foolish ones, and slow of heart to believe in all that the prophets have spoken!" Luke 24:25

Scripture records at least three instances in which Jesus forewarned His disciples about His suffering and death. For example, we read in Matthew 16:21, "From that time Jesus began to show His disciples that He must go to Jerusalem, and suffer many things from the elders and chief priests and scribes, and be killed, and be raised the third day."

Each time Jesus spoke of His death, He promised His resurrection. And yet, during the last hours of Christ's life, Judas betrayed Him; Simon Peter denied Him; and all the disciples deserted Him.

On Easter morning, instead of anticipating the risen Savior, the disciples were mourning a presumed-dead Lord. Women came to anoint a corpse. Men shuffled sadly toward Emmaus, not realizing they were talking with the resurrected Christ. On the first Easter evening, all the disciples were huddled behind locked doors. Some Easter celebration.

We may fault the disciples for their slowness to believe. But haven't we all resembled them at times; worrying, surrendering, trembling, hiding behind locked doors—as if Jesus Christ were still dead and buried instead of living and reigning?

When Jesus confronted the Emmaus disciples on the first Easter, He did not admonish them for failing to recognize Him, but rather for failing to believe what the Scriptures said about Him. "O foolish ones," He said, "and slow of heart to believe in all that the prophets have spoken!"

You and I have the same Scriptures in our possession.

SLOW TO BELIEVE

Looking back, Lord, I know that You said,
"I must suffer, die, and rise from the dead.
Death will seem to have its way,
but I will rise in triumph on the third day."

Yet, on the third day, what was I doing?
Not living Your victory, but lamenting Your losing.
And it's clear to me now from such faithless behavior,
I wasn't praising the Lord but mourning a dead Savior.

And looking back, I was not alone—
like the women who worried about rolling away the stone,
like Mary Magdalene, who in her ardor
confused You with the graveyard gardener.

Peter and John, thinking You were dead,
left Your empty tomb scratching their heads.
Doubting Thomas demanded to see
the spear-wounds and nail-prints before he'd believe.

Two disciples on their way to Emmaus,
felt as if You had failed to save us.
They wished Your crucifixion undone,
thinking, "Apparently, Jesus was not the one."

This was our worship on that first Easter night,
a worship of worry and riddled with fright,
a small congregation hiding behind locked doors,
dabbing our eyes, pacing the floor.

Suddenly, You were there in the middle of the room,
gladdening our hearts, dispelling our gloom;
showing us the wounds in Your hands and feet,
admonishing us for doubting, compelling us to believe.

Yes, looking back, Lord, I know that You said:
"I must suffer, die, and rise from the dead."
I missed the joy You wanted me to receive,
because I was quick to doubt and slow to believe.

Pack Your Suitcase, Son

"For you did not receive the spirit of bondage again to fear,
but you received the Spirit of adoption by whom we cry out,
'Abba, Father.'" Romans 8:15

I'm adopted.

On June 12, 1953, after I'd spent two and a half months in
an orphanage in Tampa, Florida, my new parents, Paul
and Carol Weis, took me home. On the day this happened,
my dad looked at me and said, "Pack your suitcase, son.
We're going home."

I've often contemplated what this selfless, loving act of
adoption brought to me: a name, home, inheritance, and
family. I can identify with the words of Paul in Romans
8:15, "...you received the Spirit of adoption by whom we cry
out, 'Abba, Father.' " The Greek word for sonship literally
means "to place as a son," that is, to adopt.

Adoption involves a deliberate choice. I did not choose my
adoptive parents; they chose me. When Paul describes us
as adopted, he's reminding us that God deliberately chose
us. God chose us because He wanted us. Our faith in Jesus
is no accident. Imagine the impact on our lives,
relationships, and careers if we began each day by saying,
"God chose me! God wanted me!"

When the Holy Spirit adopted us into God's family, He also
gave us the right to call God the Father our "Abba, Father."
Abba is an Aramaic word that means "Da-da" or "Dad." It

is a term of endearment and trust, and it's also the relationship through which Jesus taught us to pray, "Our *Father* who art in heaven."

"Pack your suitcase, son. We're going home." For me this phrase has always summarized every blessing I received through adoption. And when the time comes for us to leave this earth and claim our heavenly inheritance, I suspect we'll hear a similar phrase.

"Pack your suitcase, My child. It's time to go home."

PACK YOUR SUITCASE, SON

I don't remember the orphanage,
or the caretakers who fed and diapered me
and perhaps, when time allowed,
cradled and coddled me, wondering,
"What will become of you, little one?"

Though I don't remember,
I reflect on who and what I was;
an infant with no name,
rushed from the womb to the orphanage
and placed into the custody of strangers.

I had nothing and was nothing
other than helpless and homeless;
a pinprick in time, with no past or future,
and nothing to offer except

whimpers and tears and soiled diapers.

Yet, from such a questionable beginning,
my life became a remarkable journey of love and belonging
through the two people who rescued me,
wanted me, and said to me,
"Pack your suitcase, son. We're going home."

Adoption—
from the happy Latin word adoptare,
meaning "to choose."
And so, by adoption, I was changed from a child of
accident to a child of choice.

And through that single, undeserved act
of undeserved love, I received everything I once lacked:
a name, family, and home;
a lineage thicker than blood and roots deeper
than biology.

Over the years I've come to realize
that my life, my family, and my adoption
were not the convergence of time and chance,
but the convergence of grace and choices
that You, Lord, made in eternity.

Endless eons before You spoke
the universe into existence, Lord,
You spoke my name.
You said, "I have loved you with eternal love.
You are Mine."

So I became the child of two adoptions,
the one in eternity, the other in time;
both ordained by the same divine decree and love.
You, Lord, led my family to me.
And through that same family, Lord, I was led to You.

Through all the years and hardships,
whenever I've fallen, failed, feared, and felt
the coldness and cruelty of others,
I've never forgotten the unique joy
of being adopted.

People may hurt and reject me,
the world may scoff and ridicule me,
the devil himself may seek to rob me of joy,
but nothing and no one can change the truth of my
adoption: You, Lord, wanted me. Me.

No, I don't remember the orphanage.
But I will always remember God's love and grace.
And when the time comes to leave this life for the next,
perhaps I will hear the same words spoken long ago:
"Pack your suitcase, son. We're going home."

Wise Men

"For we have seen His star in the East and have come to worship Him." Matthew 2:2

Imagine what the wise men saw when they finally reached the infant Jesus: not a palace, but a simple house in the sleepy little town of Bethlehem; not luxuries, but the barest necessities; not a crown, but a crude cradle; not an ostentatious display of power, but a display of complete humility—a little Child, who at this time was likely less than two years old.

Yet, the wise men did not look at each other in disbelief; or recheck the position of the star and the address of the house; or say to each other, "This can't be the right place," and of Jesus, "This can't be the right king." Instead, the wise men believed. "And when they had come into the house, they saw the young Child with Mary His mother, and fell down and worshiped Him." (Matthew 2:11)

When traveling on their own, without the miraculous star, the wise men went to the wrong town, Jerusalem; and to the wrong king, Herod. But when following God's star and Word, they found Jesus. They recognized Jesus for who He was: not simply the son of Mary, but the Son of God and the Savior of mankind.

God leads us to Jesus in the same way; namely, through the light of His Word. The apostle Paul wrote to Timothy, "...from childhood you have known the Holy Scriptures, which are able to make you wise for salvation through faith which is in Christ Jesus." (2 Timothy 3:15)

Following God's Word is what made the wise men wise.
Following the Scriptures is what makes us wise, too.

WISE MEN

What makes a wise man wise?
The answer might surprise you.

It has nothing to do with universities,
intelligence quotients, or doctorate degrees;
magna cum laude or common sense,
honor roll or experience.

It's not based on human philosophy
or Einstein's Theory of Relativity;
physics, science, or mathematics;
biology, astrology, or quantum mechanics.

It's not measured in titles or accolades;
academic achievements or report card grades;
joules, amps, light intensity,
speed, mass, weight, or density.

Wisdom is knowing Jesus Christ,
His perfect obedience and sacrifice,
His miracles, teaching, and above all,
the cost He paid to save the lost.

Wisdom is knowing God's holy Word
and taking to heart what is read and heard
about creation, redemption, sin and grace,
and God's plan of salvation for the human race.

Wisdom, true wisdom, is from above.
It embraces Christ as the embodiment of God's love.
It trusts in Jesus alone for salvation,
and sees Him as the highest form of education.

Wisdom is following the same star
that led wise men to Christ from afar.
Through wisdom we come to realize
that following God's Word made the wise men wise.

What makes a wise man wise?
The answer might surprise you.

Loneliness

"I will never leave you nor forsake you." Hebrews 13:5

Many things can make us lonely: retirement, children leaving the parental "nest" for lives of their own, the death of loved ones, depression, addictions, even staring into the vastness of a night sky. And loneliness is a dreadful feeling. To quote from an old song by *Three Dog Night*: "One is the loneliest number that you'll ever do."

For me, however, the greatest loneliness I've ever known was the result of divorce—first, my parents' divorce when I was a child, and much later, my own unwanted divorces. The poem *Loneliness* was my attempt to describe that "loneliest number"—in a way, like paging through a scrapbook of painful memories.

Everything about divorce made me horribly lonely. An empty house, empty bed, empty closets. Not seeing my children daily, missing their hugs, laughter, happy chatter, crayon artwork. The haunting sound of my own footsteps in the hallway.

Hating the loneliness, sometimes I'd drive for hours, not knowing where I was going, or for that matter, where I'd been. I'd frequent the same restaurants at the same times—no one likes to cook for one or eat alone—and hear the same waitresses say, "You want the usual?" Ritual, I suppose, was my meager attempt to compensate for the loneliness.

And what made me lonelier still was my reluctance to tell anyone about what I was going through, even the closest members of my family. I did tell God, but He didn't seem too interested.

In fact, at times, I was almost certain that He had forsaken me. Only, this was never the case. Later, when I looked back through the years and tears, I realized that God had never left me and never would.

When I *thought* I was alone, He was the One walking beside me—at times, carrying me. He was the One sitting beside me at the dinner table and in the passenger seat on my long drives.

You aren't alone either. For God Himself has promised, "I will never leave you nor forsake you."

LONELINESS

Loneliness?
Yes, I understand loneliness.

Loneliness is the thick, gnawing fear
in a child's heart as he lies in bed at night,
rolled into a fetal ball,
listening to parental arguments
which sound like the end of the world.
The words are bitter.
The sobs are loud.

The terror is real.

Loneliness is the face of a ten-year-old boy
pressed against a cold glass window,
waiting for the spill of headlights on the driveway,
wondering if divorce means death,
and if losing one parent means losing both.
The glass is cold.
The house is quiet.
The wait is long.

Loneliness is an empty house
where a clock tick-tocks torturously
and a single pair of footsteps echo in the hallway
and the table is set for one
and the TV blares companionship.
The noises are haunting.
The rooms are tombs.
The memories are ghosts.

Loneliness is eating at the same restaurants
and sitting in the same booths
and hearing the same waitresses with beehive hairdos
ask the same questions: "Just one of you?"
and "You want the usual?"
The questions are painful.
The restaurants are habit.
The diners are whispering.

Loneliness is staring at crayoned artwork
and untouched toys,
and missing the patter of little footsteps in the morning

and the rush of news after school
and the sound of quiet prayers at night.
The divorce is final.
The damage is done.
The family is broken.

Loneliness is sorting through old photographs,
a drive alone through holiday lights,
a memory of better times and youthful days
when laughter came in torrents
and every story ended in "happily ever after."
The endings are different.
The laughter is fleeting.
The photographs are faded.

Loneliness is staring into the vastness
of the night sky,
and realizing how mortal
and microscopically small we are
when compared to the infinitude of the Creator.
The Creator is almighty.
The Creator is eternal.
The Creator is omniscient.

Yes, I know loneliness in all of its forms
and in all its symptoms,
and therefore find no greater comfort
than the comfort of these words of God:
"I will never leave you nor forsake you."
The comfort is real.
The words are true.
The promise is powerful.

Loneliness cannot prevail over the love of God,
the God who came to be with us,
and one of us,
and promised us, "I am with you always,
even to the end of the age."
The Savior is present.
The salvation is won.
The peace is ours.

Let the sun fail and the moon fall
and the world bellow and scowl
and false friends forsake—
God is still with me,
beside me, eternally my Immanuel.
The loneliness is gone.
The emptiness is past.
The heartache is healed.

Forget-Me-Nots

"Bless the LORD, O my soul; and all that is within me,
bless His holy name! Bless the LORD, O my soul, and forget
not all His benefits." Psalm 103:1-2

Thanksgiving is a prominent theme in Scripture. In view of God's love, forgiveness, mercy, and undeserved salvation in Jesus Christ, His people should be thankful people.

Regrettably, there is another prominent theme in Scripture: namely, forgetting about God. Whether stated negatively, "Do not forget the LORD your God," or positively, "Remember the LORD your God"; such admonitions occur more than sixty times in the Bible. Obviously, there is a strong connection between forgetfulness and thankfulness.

However, people of God forgetting about God seems unthinkable, doesn't it? But then, did the Israelites forget about God? Did the nine lepers forget about God? There are no sadder words in Scripture than these words of God in Jeremiah 2:32, "Can a virgin forget her ornaments, or a bride her attire? Yet My people have forgotten Me days without number."

"Forget not all His benefits," wrote King David. Psalm 103 does not list all the benefits of God in our lives, but it does list some of the greatest blessings—forgiveness, healing, redemption, loving-kindness, tender mercies, and daily provisions. Each of these blessings should drive us to our knees in humble, joyful thanksgiving. Think of them as

"Forget-Me-Nots."

If you are going through difficulties today; if you're struggling financially, spiritually, or emotionally; remember God's benefits to you in Jesus Christ. Consider them. Dwell on them. Write them down on paper if need be. But don't forget or overlook God's blessings in your life.

Remembering will make you thankful.

FORGET-ME-NOTS

There is a garden in my thoughts.
I call it God's Forget-Me-Nots.
Every plant found within it
is a planting of the Holy Spirit.

It is His role to water and nourish,
to make my Forget-Me-Nots grow and flourish.
He roots them in Scripture so that all my days
they bring forth abundant fruits of praise.

Forget-Me-Not how God in love
rains down blessings from above.
He is the Giver of each good gift,
the Source of all my benefits.

Forget-Me-Not God forgives my sins,
whenever I repent and trust in Him.
He removes them farther than east is from west,

and clothes me in Christ's perfect righteousness.

Forget-Me-Not God heals my diseases,
my cuts and cancers, fevers and sneezes.
He heals my body and restores my soul.
In the wounds of Christ He makes me whole.

Forget-Me-Not how God has been
my Savior from the guilt of sin.
He claimed me, cleansed me, and set me free
to be His own for eternity.

Forget-Me-Not God's mercies abound.
He took my poverty and gave me a crown.
And at that undeserved coronation,
He crowned me with loving-kindness and compassion.

Forget-Me-Not God gives good things
to make my soul rejoice and sing.
He renews me daily, and through His truth
gives me all the strength of youth.

Christ Crucified

"But we preach Christ crucified." 1 Corinthians 1:23

Paul told the Corinthians, "But we preach Christ crucified." Yet, what is more scandalous to the unbelieving world than the message of a crucified Savior? How could crucifixion bring salvation?

The cross was reserved for the vilest of criminals—an emblem of shame, not victory; pain, not healing; death, not life. In fact, our word *excruciating* is from the Latin *excruciato*, literally meaning "out of the cross."

Sadly, even some Christian churches today have stopped proclaiming the message of the cross, at least in its fullness. They fear the cross will impact membership, and membership will impact budgets. Instead, they offer mere earthly wisdom or so-called prosperity gospels or feel-good pep-talks. "God loves you," they say, not realizing that the enormity of God's love cannot be measured without the enormity of Christ's sacrifice.

Yet, from the beginning of time, "Christ crucified" has been God's message of salvation. Even in the first promise of the Savior—"I will put enmity between you and the woman, and between your seed and her Seed; He shall bruise your head, and you shall bruise His heel" (Genesis 3:15)—deliverance was linked to Christ's sacrifice.

"Christ crucified" is the sum and substance of the entire Bible—proclaimed by Old Testament prophets, New Testament apostles, and by Jesus Christ Himself, who told His disciples that He "must go to Jerusalem, and suffer many things from the elders and chief priests and scribes, and be killed, and be raised the third day." (Matthew 16:21)

We preach "Christ crucified," because there is no other Savior and no other way to be saved.

CHRIST CRUCIFIED

Loving, faithful God,
my God,
dying on a cursed tree,
dying the worst of deaths
reserved for the worst of criminals—
for failures, traitors, and slaves.
O cruel, brutal death,
which You, Son of God, willingly died.

The proud say, "Scandalous!"
The wise say, "Foolish!"
They still spit and mock
and weave crowns of thorns
and blasphemous arguments.

They still say, "Away with Jesus!
We don't want Him or need Him!

Give us another Messiah,
a manmade Messiah,
a Messiah who makes sense,
builds roads, brings peace, writes checks."

They don't see God on that tree.
They don't see the love in His pain
or the strength in His weakness
or the life in His death
or the forgiveness in His blood.
They see only foolishness.

Yet, they are the fools.
For all their taunts and titles,
degrees and demands,
insights and outbreaks,
they don't know truth or God or salvation or faith;
or why their homegrown wisdom
cannot bring peace and happiness
or answer the most nagging questions of life.

Instead, they stumble about—
nothing but blind fools in caps and gowns,
calling darkness light,
and lies truth,
and wisdom folly.

To them, "Christ crucified"
is the native language of the Ignorant
and the punchline of coffee-break jokes.

But what they call wisdom,

God calls folly.
What they call foolish,
God calls wise.
And what God calls wise
is "Jesus Christ and Him crucified."

So this is what we preach:
"Christ crucified."
Two salutary words
in one immeasurable act of love and redemption;
the undeniable evidence of Man's sin
and God's redemption.

O merciful Christ,
You who died that cruel death on the cross—
though others may mock and scorn,
preferring performance to substance
and statistics to truth;
though they may remove Your cross
from their sermons and hymns,
their creeds and alcoves,
we will preach "Christ crucified."

God's message.
God's wisdom.
God's power.

A View from the Mountaintop

"And He was transfigured before them." Matthew 17:2

Have you ever driven through mountains? Have you ever stopped at a scenic view to admire the dizzying heights and distant landscapes? The view from a mountaintop gives one a different perspective. And that which Peter, James, and John witnessed on the Mount of Transfiguration was meant to give them a different perspective; not a better view of the landscape, but a better view of their Savior, Jesus Christ.

On that day and mountain, Jesus was transfigured before His disciples. His appearance dramatically changed. The Greek word used is *META-MOR-PHO-O*, the source of our English *metamorphosis*. Matthew wrote, "His face shone like the sun, and His clothes became as white as the light." (Matthew 17:2)

For three and a half years, the disciples had witnessed Christ's glory in His words and miracles. But on the Mount of Transfiguration, if only momentarily, they glimpsed Christ's glory as God the Son. And they heard the clear testimony of God the Father: "This is My beloved Son, in whom I am well pleased. Hear Him!" (Matthew 17:5)

The transfiguration was not for the benefit of Christ; or for Moses and Elijah, who appeared with Jesus on the mountaintop; or for God the Father. Instead, it was for the benefit of the disciples of Jesus, who in dark days ahead would see Him betrayed, beaten, bleeding, and dying on a cross.

The same is true of us. What you and I witness of Christ on the sacred mountaintop of Scripture—His true deity and true humanity—is meant to strengthen and prepare us, and to go with us as we leave the mountaintop for the harsh realities of the plain.

A VIEW FROM THE MOUNTAINTOP

When I am hurting, Lord,
when I feel low, unloved, or depressed,
I leave the masses and the messes of the world behind
and climb the sacred mountaintop of Your holy Word.

On this mountaintop,
the air is bright with hope
and lifegiving with forgiveness.
From its heights,
I see the Things That Matter
and the Things That Have No Worth.

On this mountaintop,
I see the Bible for what it is,
not what skeptics call it—
fiction, fables, and fairy tales.
No, each word is the inspired work of the Holy Spirit,
the Absolute Truth by which all must be measured,
and the Final Authority before which all must bow.

On this mountaintop,
I see across the millennia to the beginning of time.
I see that the universe is not the accidental consequence of
Blind Evolution and Random Chance,
but the result of Your Word and Your will, O God.
"Let there be!" You said; and there was—
instantly, inevitably, wondrously.

On this mountaintop,
I see that I am no accident of nature,
no speck of stardust in a cold, uncaring cosmos.
I am Your creation, O God;
special, loved, unique, wanted,
given a life with purpose,
chosen in eternity to become Yours in time.

On this mountaintop,
I see what is wrong with the world;
the reason for its ills and illnesses,
wars and crimes,
heartaches and obituaries.
And the reason is sin,
a three-letter word that many churches refuse to say
for fear of emptying pews and coffers.
Yet, Your Word says it, and so I believe it.

Once, Lord Jesus, on another mountaintop,
the Mount of Transfiguration,
Peter and James and John glimpsed
Your unveiled glory as God the Son—
Your face shining like a trillion noonday suns
and Your garments growing whiter than light.

They heard the testimony of God the Father, saying,
"This is My beloved Son,
in whom I am well pleased.
Hear Him!"

But on this mountaintop,
the sacred mountaintop of Your Word,
I witness the Person of Christ
in equal clarity, indeed, with even more certainty:
Jesus Christ, true God, begotten of the Father in eternity;
Jesus Christ, true Man, born of the Virgin Mary
in the fullness of time;
Jesus Christ, our perfect Savior.

On this mountaintop,
I see the cruel cross for what it is:
the bloody instrument on which Jesus Christ
suffered and died to atone for the sins of the world—
every wrong thought,
every evil deed,
every ill-spoken word
of every human being.

On this mountaintop,
I see the risen Savior stepping forth from the sepulcher;
proving salvation and forgiveness,
offering living hope,
conquering death, devil, and hell,
and giving the guarantee of life eternal
to all who believe in Him as Lord and Savior.
His words resound with joy and comfort:
"Because I live, you will live also."

When I am hurting, Lord,
when I feel low, unloved, or depressed,
I leave the masses and messes of the world behind
and climb the sacred mountaintop of Your Word—
so that through its power, its hope, and its promises
I may return invigorated to the realities of the plain.

Majesty in Minor Matters

*"This beginning of signs Jesus did in Cana of Galilee,
and manifested His glory; and His disciples
believed in Him." John 2:11*

All of us face difficulties; and when we do, we are tempted
to doubt God's goodness, fairness, and power. We find
ourselves asking questions we hate to ask: "Where is God?
Why isn't He helping?" Christ's first miracle, as recorded
in John 2:1-11, demonstrates how God reveals His majesty
in even our minor matters.

Consider where Jesus performed His first miracle. Was it
in the capital city of Jerusalem or on the temple mount or
at the luxurious palace of King Herod? No. Jesus
performed His first miracle in the small, don't-blink-or-
you'll-miss-it village of Cana in Galilee.

Consider why Jesus performed His first miracle. Was it to
solve a world crisis or calm a tempest? No. Jesus performed
His first miracle to remedy a shortage of wine at a
wedding.

And consider for whom Jesus performed His first miracle.
Was it for a Roman governor or renowned religious
leader—the wealthy and influential of this world? No.
Jesus performed His first miracle for two newlyweds,
whose names we don't even know.

If the wedding at Cana is not proof enough of God's
involvement in our lives, then consider how Jesus Christ,

though in very nature God, humbled Himself and willingly embraced the agonizing death of the cross to atone for our sins. How "involved" is that?

God is willing to reveal His glory even in our minor matters. Sometimes, it simply takes a shortage to make us appreciate a miracle.

MAJESTY IN MINOR MATTERS

Lord, had it been up to me,
I'd have chosen a different place than Cana in Galilee
to perform my first miracle.
Why not Jerusalem or Rome,
Herod's palace or Caesar's home?
But Cana?

Had it been up to me,
I'd have chosen a different family
for my first miracle—
wealthy kings and queens,
powerful people with unlimited means;
but not a Galilean bride and groom
too poor for a honeymoon
or adequate wedding reception.

Had it been up to me,
I'd have chosen a different tragedy
to solve with my first miracle—
curing cancer, ending world hunger,

even making the elderly younger.
But a shortage of wine?
That's hardly worth the time
of the Creator of heaven and earth.

Lord, had it been up to me,
I'd have done things much differently—
or so I thought, until You let me see
the big lesson in little Cana.

You are the God of my salvation,
powerful and glorious beyond all description—
my Creator, Redeemer, and Comforter.
Yet, at times that very majesty
begs the question: "Why would You care about me;
my life, my worries, my problems?"

But this is the lesson You wanted me to see
at that wedding in Cana of Galilee—
with Your choice of first miracles.
Firsts always give a lasting impression;
and the miracle You worked at that wedding reception
was meant to fill me with hope, joy, and comfort.

Yes, You are the God of my salvation—
powerful and glorious beyond my puny comprehension.
Yet, at Cana You taught me that there is never a time
when You are unwilling to solve a little problem of mine,
like that little shortage of wine in Cana.

Persistent Prayers

"And behold, a woman of Canaan came from that region and cried out to Him, saying,, 'Have mercy on me, O Lord, Son of David! My daughter is severely demon-possessed.' But He answered her not a word." Matthew 15:22-23

In 1985 I was pastoring a small church in northern California. While outwardly happy—I became very adept at wearing a smiley face—inwardly my heart was breaking. My wife and I were heading toward divorce, and no amount of pleading on my part slowed the pace or changed the direction.

One night I was so depressed that I walked the short distance to the church building, stepped inside, and in the darkness lay down prostrate before the altar, with my nose pressed against the red industrial carpet and tears coursing down my cheeks.

"Oh, God!" I pleaded. "You are almighty! You can do anything! Please, I beg you, save my marriage!" But all I heard that dreadful night were the sounds of my own sobs and sighs echoing off the church walls.

I can sympathize with that Canaanite woman, who pleaded with Jesus to heal her demon-possessed daughter; and in response received only silence and then rebuffs from the Savior. But did she give up? Did she stop praying? No. Why?

Because she knew who Jesus was: the gracious, compassionate Savior who promised to answer our prayers at the right time and in the right way. And her trust in Him was vindicated. After the silence and rebuffs came the blessed words, "O woman, great is your faith! Let it be to you as you desire." (Matthew 15:28)

When God seems to be silent, it is only because He wants us to talk with Him. When He seems to walk away, it is only because He wants us to follow Him. And when He places obstacles in our path, it is only because He wants our faith to be a great faith.

PERSISTENT PRAYERS

"Lord, help me! Please!
Stop! Save! Hear my prayers!"

I can still hear the woman's words
pouring out in a raging torrent
of white-capped sobs and sighs.
And frankly, they irritated me.
She irritated me; in fact, all of us.

We had other things to do,
other places to go, other people to see.
Jewish people. Deserving people.
Who did this loud woman think she was?
What right did she have to address the Savior
or beg for a miracle?

She was a Gentile from the region of Syro-Phoenicia;
a most un-Jewish place
filled with mostly undeserving people.

"Stop, Lord!
Hear me, please!
I beg You!"

The whole incident was becoming an embarrassment—
people stopping, staring, pointing, smirking.
"Send the woman away!" someone urged.
And others quickly signed the petition.
I did too.

Whatever her problem,
it wasn't our problem
and certainly not the Savior's problem.

And at first, Jesus seemed to agree.
Without a word to the troublesome woman
or a recognizable glance in her direction,
the Savior pressed on.
In fact, He quickened His pace,
until her cries were lost in the banter
of crowded shops and marketplace conversations.

"Goodbye," I thought.
"Good luck.
And good riddance."
A hard occurrence, yes;
and from the woman's perspective, certain heartbreak.
But then, salvation wasn't for everyone,

and the Good Lord did not have the time
to hear and answer every prayer.

As we walked,
I began to wonder about the hour and place
of our evening meal—
surely, the Good Lord had time for that question—
when I heard the incessant clamoring begin again.

"Lord! Help me!
Don't turn from me!
Hear my prayer!"

Louder and louder, closer and closer.
"Merciful God in heaven!" I thought.
"Will this woman never fall silent?
Will she never weary of her noisome prayers?"

I was about to ask the Savior to walk faster,
when the woman brushed past me,
then James and John,
then Peter and Andrew,
then all the rest of our company—
hurrying past Jesus Himself.

Only then did she stop, turn,
and, dropping to her hands and knees,
lie face-down in the middle of the road.

"Of all the. . ." I started,
but was too stunned to go on speaking.
Rather than forsake her hope,

the diminutive Canaanite woman
had only grown more persistent in her praying.

And here she was, blocking the path of Jesus Christ—
so that if He were to go on ignoring her,
He would first have to step over her.

Jesus stopped,
motioning us to do the same.
And at this, the woman rose to her knees.
With tear-streaked cheeks and outstretched arms
she pleaded again, "Lord, help me!"
I had never heard three words of such pain and misery.

Jesus looked at her.
And when He finally spoke,
His words were not the benediction she expected.
They were cold and aloof,
filled with more obstacles than hope:
"It is not good to take the children's bread
and throw it to the little dogs," He said.

If ignoring the woman
had not ended her quest,
these words of Jesus most certainly would.
In so saying, He had blocked the progress of her prayers
as surely as she had blocked His progress on the road.

Here her quest would end.
Here the woman's prayers would die a tearful death.
Here her heart would break into countless pieces,
and on her dusty knees she would be forced to admit

that Jesus Christ was Savior of some,
but not Savior of all.

A lump rose in my throat.
I was no longer hungry.
And against my will, I began to feel compassion
for the un-Jewish woman and her sorely vexed daughter.

I wondered—not for the last time—
if the Savior had been too hard on her,
if a firm "NO" from the first prayer would have been
a better solution than hurriedly walking away
or talking of house-dogs at their master's table.

Can you see this woman;
this small, grieving mother kneeling in the road
before the Lord of heaven and earth,
her head lowered,
her eyes pooling tears,
her arms outstretched as if to embrace?

Can you see her?
I can't un-see her.
And the vision haunts me.

Yet, to my astonishment,
even then the woman refused to despair or surrender,
but threw herself upon the mercy of God
as she had thrown herself before Jesus on the road.
And amid the pain and misery in her voice,
she still said with quiet hope,
"Yes, Lord, yet even the little dogs eat the crumbs

which fall from their masters' table."

This was that precious moment
for which the Lord had waited,
and to which the Lord had led the woman—
step by step,
silence by silence,
obstacle by obstacle.

And when she had reached that moment,
the Savior said, "O Woman, great is your faith!
Let it be to you as you desire."
And her daughter was healed from that very hour.

I have often reflected on that day,
that strange walk through a crowded street,
while a heartbroken woman followed,
praying loudly and persistently,
refusing to end her petitions until the Lord of All
stopped, listened, and answered.

I have often wondered what made this woman
such a persistent prayer.
Was it a strength we don't have?
A determination we don't own?
A secret we don't know?
Jesus gave the answer:
"O woman, great is your faith!".

That small, heartbroken, un-Jewish woman
refused to stop praying—
not because of who she was,

but because of whom she knew Jesus to be:
the infinitely loving,
endlessly compassionate Savior,
who always answers our prayers
at the right time,
at the right place,
and in the right way.

Lord,
there have been many times in my own life
when I prayed for help,
but You remained silent;
when I persistently followed,
but You walked away.

Yet, thanks to Your Word
I now understand the reasons.
When You are silent, You want me to talk with You.
When You walk away, You want me to follow You.
When You place obstacles in my way,
You want my faith to be a great faith.

So, I'll go on praying,
not because of who I am,
but because of who You are –
because You're always there,
always listening,
always waiting to answer,
always desiring to give me more
than I can ask or even imagine.

Entering Another's Story

"But he, wanting to justify himself, said to Jesus,
'And who is my neighbor?'" Luke 10:29

Decades ago, my dear friend Jean and I went to see the movie *Rocky*. Jean was not a boxing fan, and expected nothing from the movie except disinterest and disgust.

But then a strange thing happened. During the final climactic scene, when Rocky was pummeled, bloodied, and all but beaten—knocked down repeatedly, yet still managing to stagger to his feet and box on—I glanced at Jean and was astonished to see her feinting, jabbing, and wincing along with Rocky. What had happened? She had entered the story. In a sense, Jean was now on the movie screen, and Rocky was sitting next to me spilling popcorn.

A story is most meaningful when we enter it; when we identify with the joys and sorrows, pleasures and predicaments of the characters. But what if that story is fact instead of fiction? What if that story is another human life: the story of a man lying forgotten in a nursing home; the story of a woman diagnosed with cancer; the story of divorce, foreclosure, job loss, or ingratitude?

How willing are we to enter these stories? How willing are we to stop, help, and get involved? Or do we prefer, like a certain priest and Levite in a certain parable, to hurriedly cross the street and pass by on the other side?

These are the questions Jesus raised in His parable of the *Good Samaritan*. Not long ago, I found myself confronted with the same nagging questions—not on the road to Jericho, but at a bench outside a supermarket in Fort Myers, Florida.

ENTERING ANOTHER'S STORY

She sat on a green metal bench
outside of the supermarket,
smoking a cigarette between sips of water
and fits of coughing:
a painfully thin woman with blonde hair,
bronzed, wrinkled skin,
and expressionless eyes that flitted
between the parking lot and her own simple shoes.

"Who is she?" I wondered.
"Why would anyone sit on a metal bench
in the Florida sun?"
Sun and smoke.
A lethal combination, I thought,
and promptly dubbed the woman
Miss Melanoma and Lady Lung Cancer.
I never learned her real name.

Each trip I made to the supermarket,
the nameless woman was there—
different clothes but same bench,
same water,

same cigarettes,
same phlegmy cough,
same sunken eyes sweeping the parking lot,
embracing shoppers who quickly passed by.

I was one of them, a passerby.
Surely, the woman wasn't my problem.
And her stare seemed as dangerous to me
as her second-hand smoke.
Yet, increasingly, each time I visited the store,
I looked for her.
Each time she looked at me.

One day I inquired about her.
"That woman who sits on the bench outside,"
I said to a smiling checkout clerk,
"what's her story?"

The clerk's smile darkened into sympathy.
"Well," she replied, "I don't know her name,"
(did anyone?)
"but I've heard that she lives in the
apartments across the street.
She comes here every day just to sit on that bench.
I think she's lonely.
Sad, you know?
That'll be twenty dollars and sixty-one cents."

One month passed,
then two, three—
then autumn and the first suggestion of winter;
and still the woman sat,

looking and sipping, smoking and coughing.

And each time I saw her, Lord,
each time I told myself that very soon now,
tomorrow, surely the day after that,
I'd sit down on that green bench next to her
and introduce myself.
I'd stop, smile, and ask the woman
if she needed anything;
and maybe tell her about You.

But something always intervened,
something important,
like making sure the ground beef was fresh
and that the coffee was on sale.

And then one day,
the green metal bench was empty.
The woman was gone, just gone—
perhaps tired of sitting,
tired of the supermarket,
tired of the indifferent shoppers,
tired of living.
I don't know and I never asked.
I simply passed by on the other side.

No, I didn't know the woman's name or her story.
I judged the book by its cover
and had no interest in reading more—
until there was no more to read.
And somehow, the bench, the parking lot,
and the whole world seem emptier because of it.

The bench is still there; the woman is not.
Each time I pass it I wonder
if that lonely woman ever knew how much
You, Lord, loved her;
if she ever knew that You, Lord, had redeemed her.

Most of all,
I wonder why I never stopped long enough to tell her.
I just kept passing by.

Time Flies

"The days of our lives are seventy years; and if by reason of strength they are eighty years, yet their boast is only labor and sorrow; for it is soon cut off, and we fly away." Psalm 90:10

Once upon a time. . . I was riding in the car with my dad, when he suddenly became uncharacteristically somber. Looking at me, he patted my skinny knee and said, "Son, *tempus fugit.*" I replied, "Tempus what-it?" He repeated, "*Tempus fugit*. That's Latin for 'time flies.'"

At ten years old, I had no serious concept of flying time. The one image that came to mind was that of a cartoonish alarm clock with wings, doing loop-the-loops in my bedroom. Funny, sure. But judging by the look on dad's face, *tempus fugit* was not meant to make me laugh.

"Time flies," he said again. "One minute you're young, the next you're"—his voice trailed off to silence. Then he added, "And the older you get, the faster time flies." A moment later, we were laughing and joking and eventually singing a song dad learned during World War II; something like "Oh, the coffee in the army they say is mighty fine. It's good for cuts and bruises and tastes like iodine."

I never forgot that song; and I never forgot that expression—*tempus fugit*, though it took several decades for me to understand the true meaning of flying time. And Dad, you were right. Time flies. Time flees like a bandit, stealing away youth, looks, thoughts, and loved ones. You

127

were also right about time speeding up as one ages. Why this happens, I don't know. Every minute has sixty seconds, and every hour has sixty minutes.

Yet, as if by some strange magic, the older I've grown, the faster time has flown. I should be turning eleven, not sixty-five. The face in the mirror should be my grandfather's, not mine. But it's me—less hair, longer nose, bigger ears.

Yet, despite the brevity and fragility of our lives, God the Holy Spirit has stretched our little lifetimes to all the dimensions of eternity by leading us to faith in our Savior, Jesus Christ. Through Christ, eternal life is not only something we anticipate; it is something we already own.

As Jesus said, "Most assuredly, I say to you, he who hears My word and believes in Him who sent Me has everlasting life, and shall not come into judgment, but has passed from death into life." (John 5:24)

TIME FLIES

Where did the time go?
I don't know.
I don't know.

One day I was young, having fun,
laughing and playing in the Florida sun,
running barefoot over grass so green,
catching butterflies, chasing dreams.

Then I was old.
How?
I don't know.
I don't know.

Once my hair was brown and thick,
my grip was strong, my mind was quick.
Now I'm wrinkled everywhere.
My head displays more scalp than hair.
When I look in a mirror all I see
is a parody of what I used to be.
How?
I don't know.
I don't know.

Once all my friends and I
lived as though we'd never die.
We raced our bikes, leaped from trees,
stubbed our toes, scraped our knees.
Now we're all fading away,
like a dimming sunset at the end of day.
How?
I don't know.
I don't know.

I remember when TV was black and white,
when people said "groovy" and "outta sight"—
the Beverly Hillbillies, Mr. Magoo,
Leave It to Beaver, Ed Sullivan too;
Billy Jean King versus Bobby Riggs;
Kennedy, Kruschev, the Bay of Pigs;
the Beatles, Animals, Eagles, and Stones;

Woodstock, Watergate, and party-line phones.

I remember the days my two sons were born;
how I held and cradled them in my two arms.
Now both are full-grown, too big for my knee.
I'm as proud of them as a father can be.

So many years have passed me by
without stopping, turning, or waving goodbye.
Where did the time go?
I don't know.
I don't know.

You, O Lord, are from eternity.
Why do You care for a mortal like me,
when my lifespan is measured in years and hours,
and my glories fade like withering flowers?

You are the Alpha and Omega, the Beginning and End;
yet You've loved me, saved me, and called me Your friend.
Through all the changes, through all the years,
You've been at my side, drying my tears.

You've blessed me beyond all expectation,
sacrificed Your Son to win my salvation.
Your constant, faithful love for me
has covered my time with eternity.
And when my days on earth are done,
I will share in the glories yet to come.
This I do know.
How?
You, O God, have told me so.

Case Number J81-11

"And Jesus said to her, 'Neither do I condemn you; go and sin no more.'" John 8:11

I've come to think of John 8:1-11 as Case Number J81-11; that is, the account of a woman accused of adultery, rushed from her bedroom to the courtroom of public opinion, condemned, then brought to Jesus for His judgment—at His feet finding mercy instead of condemnation.

While we are drawn to this case for many reasons: Pharisees failing in their plot to discredit Jesus; accusers dropping stones and returning home; the powerful image of the adulterous woman lying in the street, embarrassed, bereft of dignity and hope, weeping, expecting to die— surely, it is the forgiveness of the Savior that draws us the most.

In a real sense, we have all been like that poor woman: "caught in the act" of sinning against God; shown the same undeserved love and forgiveness; blessed with the same precious words, "Neither do I condemn you; go and sin no more."

Scripture not only teaches the difference between Law and Gospel in "proof passages." It also teaches this important difference within the context of real flesh and blood, real human problems, real human failings—like Case Number J81-11, where the Law showed an adulterous woman her sin, and the Gospel liberated her with the reality of forgiveness in Christ.

Of course, if we do not see ourselves as sinful, then we do not understand the Law of God any better than the Pharisees. And if we insist on throwing stones at contrite sinners, who have repented of their sins and asked for forgiveness, then we do not understand the Gospel of God either, or how much we ourselves have been forgiven.

CASE NUMBER J81-11

They rushed the woman from the bedroom
to the Courtroom of Public Opinion,
casting her like refuse at the feet of Jesus.

There she lay,
half-clad and wholly broken,
hair in tangles,
eyes streaming tears,
with no one to defend her
and no defense to be made.
She was guilty.

Those who brought her were Pharisees—
white-washed sepulchers
full of deceit and decomposition.

Dressed in long robes and gaudy self-righteousness,
they pointed and accused:
"Harlot!"
"Homewrecker!"
"Sinner!"

"Caught in the act of adultery!"
"Worthy of death!"
And amid their accusations, this one question:
"What say You, Jesus of Nazareth?"

But Jesus said nothing.
Stooping, He began to write on the ground—
to write with the same finger of God
with which He expelled demons
and once shaped worlds.

The Pharisees waited,
but no answer came.
The sun blazed.
A bird chirped.
Far away a dog barked.
And still the Pharisees waited—
mumbling, shifting uneasily, exchanging glances.
Had this Jesus not heard them?
Was He ignoring them?

They moved closer, spoke louder:
"Rabbi, did you not hear us?
This wretched woman was caught committing adultery,
caught in the very act!
By the Law of Moses, she must be stoned.
What say You?"

A large crowd was gathering,
drawn by the loud condemnations
and the prospect of dispensing justice in the street.

As they listened, the onlookers began
searching for stones—
large stones,
jagged stones,
stones that fit the palm and fit the crime,
stones ideal for hurting and punishing
and ridding the town of homewreckers and harlots.

Amid the commotion and accusations,
the woman lay in the street,
nearly forgotten,
silently weeping and waiting to die.

"Rabbi!" the Pharisees demanded.
"Speak to us.
What say You of this filthy harlot?
You've heard our testimony.
Now render Your verdict."

Slowly, the Judge of All the Earth stood,
enveloping the accusers with eyes so deep and penetrating
that they nearly fell into them.
"If anyone of you is without sin," said Jesus,
"let him be the first to cast a stone."
Then, stooping down again, He continued to write on the
ground with the finger of God.

Suddenly, mumbling became silence;
silence, introspection;
introspection, remorse.
If anyone of you is without sin. . .
Anyone.

An old man with wispy white hair
glanced at Jesus, then at the woman,
then let the stone slip through his brittle fingers.
Another did the same.
Still another.

And one by one, the members
of the Courtroom of Public Opinion
dropped their stones
and dropped their accusations,
then returned home.

Now only two remained in the street:
Jesus and the woman,
the Savior and the sinner.

Standing again, Jesus took the woman's hand
and helped her to her feet.
Under His gaze, the woman felt more exposed than
she had ever been.
But she also felt a warmth and understanding
she had never known.

"Woman," said Jesus. "Where are your accusers?
Where are those who condemned you?"
She answered, "There are none, Lord."
He told her, "Neither do I condemn you;
go and sin no more."

Only then did the woman dare to look at her Benefactor –
dare to really look at Him.

And she found Him smiling at her,
seeing her not for what she had been
but for what His love and mercy had made her.

Over the years, so many had used and abused her,
had despised her for the harlot and homewrecker she was.
But here was the God who had undeservedly forgiven her,
the God who had defended her
when she had no defense to make.

O Lord,
I know this town, that street.
I've been there as part of the crowd,
whether as a self-righteous Pharisee hurling accusations
or as an eager bystander hurling stones.

But most of all,
I've been like that poor woman,
caught in the act of sinning—
sinning against others, sinning against You,
wrongly living and rightly condemned.

Yet, falling at Your feet in tears,
contrition, and repentance,
I've also heard You speak the same words:
"Neither do I condemn you;
go and sin no more."

So often I've wondered what
You wrote on the ground that day.
But now I'm certain of the answer.

When that harlot and homewrecker fell at Your feet,
You, the only One who had a right to cast a stone,
stooped down, and with the finger of God wrote:

FORGIVEN.

Elijah's Juniper Tree

"But he himself went a day's journey into the wilderness, and came and sat down under a broom tree. And he prayed that he might die, and said, 'It is enough! Now, LORD, take my life, for I am no better than my fathers!'" 1 Kings 19:4

Have you ever felt like giving up—like saying, "I've had enough?" At one point in his life, the prophet Elijah felt the same. Fleeing into the desert, he slumped beneath a juniper tree and begged God to end his life. "It is enough!" he said. "Now, LORD, take my life; for I am no better than my fathers!"

How could Elijah sink into such despair? He was a prophet of God. His very name expressed confidence in God: *EL-I-YAH* in Hebrew, meaning "My God is Jehovah." Yet, this was the same prophet who ran for his life from wicked Queen Jezebel and prayed for death while lying beneath a juniper tree. Why?

Elijah was not only a great prophet, he was also a human being with human weaknesses. James wrote of him, "Elijah was a man with a nature like ours." (James 5:17) Frankly, I find this very comforting—not Elijah's weakness but his humanity, the fact that he needed God as much as we do.

When things did not go as Elijah expected, he gave up. He thought, "What's the use?" He forgot what God had done for him in the past, or brushed the past aside as irrelevant to his present circumstances.

138

Yet, while we hurry to criticize Elijah, are we not like him in many ways? Amid our own problems, have we not also forgotten God's past dealings with us, or considered them totally irrelevant to our current circumstances? And so we run. We hide. We slump beneath our personal juniper tree, wondering who will help us and certain no one can.

Amid such fear and dismay, the one reality we need to remember more than any other is God's past dealings with us in Jesus Christ. For if God did not withhold the life of His own Son, but sacrificed Him to atone for our sins—will He withhold any other blessing from us: a loaf of bread, a change of clothes, a source of income, a happy marriage? No. Focusing on God's grace in Jesus Christ will empower us to stop asking "what if" and to start confessing "no matter what."

So stand up. Brush yourself off. Leave the dismal shade of the juniper tree. And live the confident, triumphant life God has given you in Jesus Christ.

ELIJAH'S JUNIPER TREE

Sometimes, I feel like giving up,
like saying, "Life is useless; I've had enough!"
Pursued by relentless misery,
I hurry to Elijah's juniper tree
and slump down.

The ground is hard and littered with stones,

with headaches, heartbreaks, and dead-dream bones.
Still, I come here anyway
to wallow in pity and eventually pray,
"Enough, Lord! Take my life!"

This juniper grows in desolation,
amid tears, toils, and tribulations.
Its trunk is twisted; its nettles are thin.
Its roots drink deeply of the depression I'm in.
Such deep depression.

Curse this dreadful juniper tree!
It won't release its hold on me.
Nor will I easily let go of it.
Instead, I prefer to sit
in its dismal shade.

Yet, though I often fret and whine,
I'm here by choice, not God's design.
My Savior died to set me free—
not chain me to this juniper tree
in hopeless surrender.

God Himself has taught me how
to leave this juniper's oppressive boughs
by turning to His holy Word
and taking to heart what I've read and heard,
the truths that set me free.

When slumped beneath this juniper tree,
I should be thinking about God, not thinking about me:
His almighty power and smiling face,

His redemptive love and the amazing grace
in which He redeemed me from my sins.

Amid my hardships, I forget to ask,
"Has God ever failed me in the past?"
And if the answer is clearly "No!"
why do I continue to doubt Him so—
doubt that He will save me now?

And even when things have not gone my way,
the outcome has always led me to say,
"Thank you, God, for what You had in mind.
Your plans for me are infinitely better than mine."
You are always at work in my life.

So, yes, sometimes I feeling like giving up,
like saying, "Life is useless; I've had enough!"
Yet, the means to overcome Elijah's juniper tree
is the tree God planted on Calvary:
the cross of Jesus Christ.

Behind the Scenes

"...the eyes of your understanding being enlightened; that you may know what is the hope of His calling, what are the riches of the glory of His inheritance in the saints, and what is the exceeding greatness of His power toward us who believe, according to the working of His mighty power." Ephesians 1:18-19

Most of us are familiar with the 1939 classic *Gone with the Wind* by Margaret Mitchell: the burning of Atlanta and memorable lines like "fiddle-dee-dee" and "tomorrow will be another day." However, many of the behind-the-scenes realities are almost as fascinating as the movie itself.

For example, the burning of Atlanta was actually the burning of old movie sets at MGM Studios in Culver City, California. Vivien Leigh, who played Scarlet O'Hara, worked on the movie for one hundred and twenty days, and afterwards received the sum of twenty-five thousand dollars. Clark Gable never wanted the role of Rhett Butler, because he viewed *Gone with the Wind* as too much of a ladies' film.

There are always behind-the-scenes realities; that is, realities that must be revealed to be known. This is true of movies, and it also true of life. When we look at our crazed, chaotic world—wars, riots, terrorism, bloodthirsty dictators, deadly diseases, natural disasters, unspeakable crimes, mass shootings—we may wrongly conclude that God has abdicated His throne. Looking at the Christian Church or our personal lives may lead us to the same conclusion.

However, the reality is much different. This world is God's world. It does not belong to Satan, Putin, Kim Jung Un, or ISIS. God is always in control. God is always governing. God is always at work in the lives of His beloved people, forcing even the worst circumstances to serve their best interests.

These are the behind-the-scenes realities revealed by Scripture. We don't always see them with the eyes in our head; rather, as Paul reminded the Ephesians, we see and believe them with the eyes of our heart.

BEHIND THE SCENES

O Lord,
when I look at the world,
I see a place of mindless messiness,
a place where wickedness abounds,
truth is relative,
and wrong is right.

Terrorists maim and murder with hellish delight,
then place their bloody handiwork online
for even children to see.
Their preaching is sword, not Spirit;
submission, not peace;
death, not life.

Dictators salute goose-stepping soldiers

and proudly display gleaming missiles;
yet, behind the parades and cameras,
they starve their own people and fill mass graves.
By day they slaughter.
At night they dream of nuclear annihilation.

There are senseless shootings,
unspeakable crimes,
corrupt politicians,
natural disasters,
blood and bullets,
deaths and obituaries.

And such hate,
ebbing and flowing, writhing and foaming
like dirty breakers on the seashore—
so that millions despise millions
for no other reason
than the color of their skin.

O Lord,
when I look at the Christian Church,
it seems so small, so helpless,
when compared to the
collective forces and loud voices
of its many foes.

Satan rages from without
and poisons from within.
So-called scholars attack Scripture
with knives of "higher criticism"—
cutting and whittling

like butchers carving meat.

And far too often,
churches which bear the name of Christ
no longer preach Christ
or the darkness of sin
or the brightness of grace—
but worry instead over income and camera angles.

To curry favor and fill pews,
they twist truth,
ignore sin,
abuse grace,
profane God,
and in so doing starve hearts.

O Lord,
when I look at my own life,
I sometimes grow doubtful and afraid—
who I am,
what I've done,
where I've been.

I'm older now,
with more years behind
than still lie ahead;
and with more aches and pains
than I care to admit,
even to myself.

Late some nights,
the beating of my own heart

sounds like the ticking
of some Cosmic Clock,
which one day will chime for me
and then grow silent.

I've lived long enough now
to realize the fragility of life,
the heartbreak of loss,
the pain of parting,
the fear of failing,
and the fear of succeeding.

Some days I'm swarmed
by clouds of "what ifs"—
dreadful creatures which bite and sting
like pesky insects:
"What if this happens?"
"What if that happens?"

And despite all my years,
all my experience,
all my study,
all my knowledge of Your love and faithfulness,
and how in Christ You gave me Your very best –
I go on expecting Your very worst.

Help me, O Lord!
Don't let me grow cold and hopeless
by what I see in this world, in the Church,
or in my personal circumstances.
Instead, open the eyes of my hurting heart
so I can see beyond appearances to realities.

Let me see the reality of the hope
to which You have called me;
the reality of the inheritance that awaits me;
the reality of the omnipotent power,
always present, ever working behind the scenes
to serve my best interests.

Let me live in the reality
that this world is Yours,
that the Christian Church is Yours,
that I am Yours,
that the glory and praise are Yours
both now and forever. Amen.

An Unexpected Ending

"Also He spoke this parable to some who trusted in themselves
that they were righteous, and despised others:
'Two men went up to the temple to pray, one
a Pharisee and the other a tax collector.'" Luke 18:9-10

Have you ever read a novel with a completely unexpected ending; an ending that left you stunned, shaking your head, and thinking, "I never saw that coming"? The people who heard Jesus tell the *Parable of the Pharisee and Tax Collector* may have felt the same.

Most of the listeners were likely Pharisees; as Luke described them, "some who trusted in themselves that they were righteous, and despised others." As such, they were no doubt thrilled with the premise of Christ's parable: two men praying in the temple, one a Pharisee, the other a tax collector or publican. From their perspective, any story about a Pharisee would have to be a good story with a happy ending—an ending in which the Pharisee was praised and the tax collector was condemned.

Only, that's not how the parable ended. According to Jesus, the tax collector "went down to his house justified rather than the other." (Luke 18:14) And at this, the listeners were stunned, disappointed, even angry. "This is not the ending we expected," they mumbled. They did not expect God to reject the religious Pharisee and forgive the sinful tax collector. But He did.

God's ways are not our ways. And His way to salvation is very different from Man's way. In the unexpected ending of this parable, Jesus taught that salvation is not based on who we are, but on who God is; not on our works, but on God's redemptive work in Jesus Christ.

In Christ we poor sinners also have an unexpected ending, a glorious ending that we had no right or reason to expect: the forgiveness of sins and eternal salvation. And that is one unexpected ending that will never disappoint us.

AN UNEXPECTED ENDING

Two men went up to the temple to pray.
One stood in a spotlight, the other in shade.

The first man was a Pharisee
convinced of his superiority.
Arrogant, insolent, and religiously dressed,
he boasted of his own righteousness:

"God, I thank You that I'm not like other men,
especially like this Publican.
I fast. I'm faultless. And don't forget,
I give a tenth of all I get.
I'm worthy of salvation, as You can plainly see.
You must be very proud of me."

But the Publican stood far away,
with no idea what to say.

He had cheated, lied, stolen, and abused—
sins for which he offered no excuse.

Unable to look heavenward, he smote his chest,
and in a tear-choked voice humbly confessed,
"God, I'm the worst of sinners, as You can plainly see.
I'm unworthy of salvation. Have mercy on me."

Which man went home justified,
the man who boasted, or the man who cried;
the man who professed superiority,
or the man who begged, "God, have mercy on me"?

In a human story, it would be the Pharisee.
But God does things differently.
In His kingdom, works don't save.
What saves is His amazing grace.

Feeling Worthless

"I wait for the LORD, my soul waits,
And in His word I do hope." Psalm 130:5

Anyone can struggle with low self-esteem and feelings of worthlessness. "Oh, I can't do anything right. I don't have what it takes. I'm useless. I hate myself. I wish I had never been born." Dismal expressions like these can become self-fulfilling prophecies. People who expect to fail usually do fail. And with each failure, low self-esteem sinks even lower.

Many factors can contribute to feelings of worthlessness: failure, loss, divorce, criticism, lack of recognition, and especially comparisons with others. "I'm not as wealthy. I'm not as attractive. I'm not as successful, likeable, tall, talkative, educated. I must be worthless."

Where should we turn when feeling worthless? When I typed the words "how to overcome low self-esteem" into an internet search engine, I got nearly three million responses of "do this" and "try that" and "avoid this" and "believe that"—when Scripture repeatedly directs us to the one true God and the answers in His one inspired Word. "In His word I do hope," wrote the psalmist.

Do you struggle with feelings of worthlessness? Then hurry to God's Word. You'll find that you are a special creation of God, not an accident of nature—as unique as your fingerprints, retinal pattern, and DNA.

God placed you here to find fulfillment in Him, to realize His great purposes for your life, and to serve others. Along with this, God adopted you into His family. Think about that. If God adopted you, God chose you. And if God chose you, God wanted you. Above all, God conferred immeasurable worth on you through the sacrifice of Jesus Christ.

If the value of something is determined by the price paid to obtain it, imagine how special and important you are to God, knowing that He paid for your redemption with the priceless blood of His own Son.

FEELING WORTHLESS

When I look at you, my heart breaks.
I see the pain in your eyes,
the weight on your shoulders,
the surrender in your steps.

Even on the brightest of days,
you seem to walk in shadow.
Your sighs speak volumes.
Your voice is the weariness of a battlefield.

I weep for you,
knowing that you have no idea
how wonderful you are—
how handsome, gifted, intelligent.

You could do anything, be anything.
But instead, you make dark predictions like
"trying is useless" and "life is pointless"—
things that cut my heart and make it bleed.

I pray for your happiness,
for the day when you will realize
how loved and wanted you are,
how important and special.

But hurt has blinded you
to your own worth,
eating at you like gangrene—
eating your will, not your flesh.

Listen!
Listen to me!
I speak the truth in Christ,
and God's Word is my witness.

You say, "I'm invisible.
No one sees me.
No one cares.
I should never have been born."

Don't you see?
You are no accident—
no collision of space and time,
molecules and minutiae.

You are a special creation of God,
as unique as your fingerprints,

placed here at this time
to live a life of joy, meaning, and purpose.

There are billions of others—
but only one you:
the you God made.
The you the world cannot do without.

And as a creation of God,
you can find fulfillment only in God—
not in fame or fortune or possessions.
Only God can fill the God-sized hole in your heart.

You say, "I want to be rich."
You mean, "I want the riches of God's grace."
You say, "I want to be loved."
You mean, "I want God's love."

And you are loved by God—
personally, infinitely, unconditionally;
a love that will make you grow, thrive, laugh, and live,
if you will only let it.

A love beyond our ability to describe
and your capacity to doubt,
if you will only look at the cross where
God wrote "I love you" in the blood of His only Son.

Others may look past you or through you,
ignore and underestimate you,
ridicule your accomplishments
or question your worth.

But to God you are of immense worth—
worth that He Himself
conferred upon you
in the priceless blood of Christ.

Along with everything else,
God adopted you into His family.
If He adopted you, He wanted you.
If He wanted you, how can you feel worthless?

When I see your pain, I weep.
But one day soon, I will share your joy—
the day you finally realize, dear loved one,
of what immense worth you are to God.

Stop, Think, Thank

"Were there not ten cleansed? But where are the nine? Were there not any found who returned to give glory to God except this foreigner?" Luke 17:17-18

Ten lepers were healed, but only one gave thanks. The other nine hurried away without a backward glance or a solitary "thank you." What differentiated the one from the nine? According to the evangelist Luke, "And one of them, when he saw that he was healed, returned, and with a loud voice glorified God, and fell down on his face at His feet, giving Him thanks." (Luke 17:15-16)

Certainly, the other nine lepers saw that they too had been healed. But that was all they saw. They did not look beyond the miracle to the Miracle Worker, Jesus Christ. Had the nine lepers viewed their healing in the same way the one had viewed his, all ten would have returned to praise Jesus. All ten would have shouted "thank you, God!" in the same loud voice with which they pleaded for Christ's mercy.

When we don't feel thankful, perhaps we are no longer seeing the blessings all around us or tracing them to their Source. However, if we take the time to stop and think, we will find countless reasons to thank. Stop and think about what?

What of the fact that the most important and lasting blessings in our lives have nothing to do with material wealth or bank accounts? The love of family and friends.

Our health. The sun that warms the day. The rain that waters the crops. The air that fills our lungs. Our bodies so wonderfully made: ears to hear, eyes to see, tongues to speak, arms to hug. These blessings are all around us and always present—blessings that all the money in the world cannot buy, yet are freely given to us by God.

Of all the blessings we have to count and count upon, surely the greatest is the eternal love of God that moved Him to give His only-begotten Son, that "whoever believes in Him should not perish but have everlasting life." (John 3:16) Who can stand beneath the cross of Jesus and still say, "I have no reason to be thankful"?

Stop and think, and you will thank.

STOP, THINK, THANK

Ten lepers were healed by Christ that day;
one gave thanks, nine walked away.
While we condemn the nine for their apathy,
do we act all that differently?

Do we thank God for every meal,
for His constant love, for the way He heals,
for the grace in which He forgives our sins
and rescues us from the troubles we're in?

Do we thank God for our family,
for blessing them so abundantly,

for our wonderful children and loving spouse,
for our job, income, health, and house?

Do we thank God for our faculties,
our reason, mind, and abilities;
for the daily blessings He faithfully imparts:
each breath we take, each beat of our heart.

Do we thank God for the sun and rain,
for flowers, fruits, vegetables, and grain;
for the amazing, beautiful world He made,
for oceans, mountains, trees, and shade?

Do we thank God for the gift of His Word,
for pastors, teachers, the sound preaching we've heard;
and most of all, for sending His Son—
for the salvation His blood and righteousness won?

I can't speak for you, only for me;
yet, this much I see with perfect clarity:
I'm simply not thankful most of the time.
I'm less like the one and more like the nine.

Changes

"The LORD is my light and my salvation; whom shall I fear?
The LORD is the strength of my life;
of whom shall I be afraid?" Psalm 27:1

Change is a part of life. In a real sense, change defines life. Every living thing is a changing thing. As human beings, we grow up, grow out, grow older, and—we hope—grow wiser. The photographs in our high school yearbooks make our children laugh. "Dad, is that really you? You were so thin, so handsome. You had so much hair."

If asked to share the story of your life, you would likely do so by describing the changes in your life. "I moved to this address. I accepted this job. I attended this church. I got married and had children. I became ill and recovered. I retired, went on a cruise, celebrated my fiftieth wedding anniversary. I buried a dearly loved spouse." Changes.

And changes, even when anticipated and welcome, can be very frightening. Our daily routines, from eating the same cereal each morning to going to bed at the same time each night, make us feel safer, more in control of our lives and world.

Change often brings uncertainty. What will happen next? Will I be better off or worse, happier or sadder, a success or a failure? We never stop asking these questions because we never stop changing. And if we had to face changes alone, we would have every reason to fear.

But as God's people, we are never alone—never at the mercy of our adversities or adversaries. God is always with us. And that never changes, because He never changes. Tell me, can you think of anything more comforting than a changeless God in a constantly changing world?

I can't either.

CHANGES

Changes.
So many changes, Lord.
My life keeps changing and rearranging
in ways I cannot foresee, fathom, or control:
ups and downs,
health and sickness,
successes and failures.

My world is changing, too.
I remember a far simpler time:
family meals,
front-porch conversations,
homemade ice cream,
black-and-white TV
with only three channels and two rabbit ears.

But that world has moved on,
nearly tripping in its haste
to kill common sense
and demonize truth—

more advanced,
more evil,
more advanced at evil.

It is a world of mass destruction,
glorified violence,
free license,
instant gratification,
scratch-off-happiness,
microwaveable love,
sexting, stalking, catfishing.

Each day death and destruction
stream into my living room
in high definition and thirty-second sound bites.
Nations rage.
Bombs drop.
Bullets fly.
Blood spills.

I see dreadful images I cannot forget:
flashing lights,
screaming sirens,
endless cemeteries,
blood-soaked battlefields,
flag-draped coffins,
starving children.

I'm changing too, Lord.
My childhood seems only an eyeblink past,
the quick turn of a page
in an unfinished novel titled "Me".

When I was young, each day lasted an eternity.
Death was only a word
that dissipated in the bright sunshine.

But somehow, as if by sinister magic,
I've grown old and obsolete,
bifocaled and sun-spotted.
The photographs in my yearbooks
make my children laugh at the difference
between Now and Then.
"Is that really you, Dad?" they ask.

"Yes," I tell them. "It's really me,
at least on the inside."
But time has changed the outside
the way tides erode the shore:
grain by grain, wave by wave;
never changing the essence,
ever reshaping the appearance.

I've known happiness and grief,
marriage and divorce,
confidence and doubt,
sickness and health,
poverty and wealth:
a two-story home in the suburbs
and a dingy one-bedroom apartment in the city.

And for me,
death is no longer an empty word
of unpleasant pronunciation.
I hear it in the ticking of clocks.

I feel it in the loss of loved ones.
I read it in the obituaries of friends.
And I know that one day it will come for me.

Changes.
So many changes and rearranges,
transitions and transpositions.
Changes for the better.
Changes for the worse.
And how frightened I would be
if I had to face these changes alone.

But I am not alone—
not for one instant,
not in one problem.
For You, Lord, are always with me;
the everlasting "I AM" of my time and eternity.
And therefore I am never at the mercy
of adversaries or adversities.

Instead, I raise my arms in utter defiance.
I shout, "The Lord is my light and my salvation;
whom shall I fear?
The Lord is the strength of my life;
of whom shall I be afraid?"
Tell me, whom?
Cancer? Loss? Loneliness? Failure? Death?

Never!
I will fear no one.
I will fear no thing.
For You, the eternal "I AM",

go before me, follow behind me,
and envelope me in Your endless love
and infinite strength.

And You, Lord, never change.
You are never for me one day
and against me the next.
You are never tired or moody,
irritable or indifferent.
You love me in good times and still love me
through bad times—from infancy to eternity.

Changes.
So many, many changes,
My life keeps changing and rearranging
in ways I cannot foresee or control.
But You, O Lord, are eternally the same—
my unchanging God
in a constantly changing world.

When God Disciplines

"Now no chastening seems to be joyful for the present, but
painful; nevertheless, afterward its yields
the peaceable fruit of righteousness to those who
have been trained by it." Hebrews 12:11

When I was a boy, no phrase worried me more than "you just wait till your father gets home." And wait I did, peeking through the curtains while contemplating my fate. Would I receive a lecture or a spanking; and if a spanking, would dad use The Belt?

As soon as dad's car pulled into our driveway, I scrambled to my room, closed the door, sat down on the bed, and acted like a cherub. "Who me? No, of course not, Dad. I would never do such a thing."

My one hope was that Dad would be too tired or too busy to discipline me. But he never was. Whether he scolded or spanked, I always got what I deserved. And it always hurt. But over the years I realized that my dad disciplined out of love, and that his discipline helped shape me into the person I am.

Should we expect anything less from our Father in heaven? Of course not. When He disciplines, He does so in absolute love and with great purpose; namely, to strengthen, train, and instruct us, so that we can run the race marked out for us with great stamina and perseverance.

To quote the writer of Hebrews: "Now no chastening seems to be joyful for the present, but painful; nevertheless, afterward it yields the peaceable fruit of righteousness to those who have been trained by it."

WHEN GOD DISCIPLINES

When I find myself in trouble,
I play a little game.
I view myself as faultless
and give God all the blame.

I ask, "God, why is this happening?
What are You putting me through?
I thought You said You loved me.
Don't You have better things to do?"

Yet, if I am truly honest,
I have no trouble proving
that many of my problems
are the result of my own doing.

I make foolish plans,
hurry down foolish roads,
listen to foolish advice,
abide in foolish abodes.

And when each act of foolishness
has brought its consequence,
I have nothing left to blame

but my own indifference.

Yet, God is my heavenly Father,
Who loves me determinedly;
and does whatever needed
in His eternal care for me.

When I do wrong, He disciplines,
as any father would—
that I may learn obedience
and "grow up" as I should.

He never sends me evil,
but will force even it
to serve my best interests
and accomplish what is fit.

Discipline is always painful.
I'd never call it fun.
But when the Almighty disciplines me
He's proving that I'm His son.

By disciplining, God strengthens me
and reveals His love and grace,
ensuring I reach the finish line
at the end of my Christian race.

So, rather than blaming God
for the trouble I may be in,
perhaps I should be thanking Him
for caring enough to discipline.

Made in the USA
Lexington, KY
20 October 2018